In **DEFENSE** of the
Word of Faith

TIMOTHY SIMS

authorHOUSE®

AuthorHouse™
1663 Liberty Drive, Suite 200
Bloomington, IN 47403
www.authorhouse.com
Phone: 1-800-839-8640

First published by AuthorHouse 11/13/2008

ISBN: 978-1-4389-1824-2 (sc)
ISBN: 978-1-4389-1823-5 (hc)

Printed in the United States of America
Bloomington, Indiana

This book is printed on acid-free paper.

Preface

There are several essential points that I hope to establish in this book. The first is that God has given to the body of Christ a member that has proven to be a true blessing. It is called the charismatic community and the Word of Faith movement. I will also express my appreciation and concerns about this member of the body of Christ that has come under critical fire and constant attack. My goal is to make a good case for the overall positive impact that this gift from God has had upon on my life. And I hope to present a solid argument for its contributions to the local church and the Universal Church at large.

Next, I will attempt to evaluate some of the criticism that surrounds the movement and to suggest some necessary changes that must take place if we want to remain a useful and valuable member of the Universal Church for end time ministry. It is not my intent to present myself as another know-it-all Bible scholar that with an opinion about what is wrong in the body of Christ today. But rather, as a fellow lay-leader, I wish to share with the reader what the Lord has taught me through experience, as I grew up in the Church and in the charismatic community. My prayer is that members of the charismatic community who have been wounded by the constant attacks upon their faith can find comfort and hope, as we explore evidence that lends credibility to support the charismatic position, in the faith.

I hope to sound the alarm and present a call for action to individuals who are recognized as leaders within the charismatic community. The purpose of this call is to acknowledge the need for a clear voice that will address the criticism and speak on behalf of this community and the Charismatic Renewal that God began over forty years ago. It is time for us to set right the wrongs within our community and address the critics and the controversy with a loving, spiritually mature apologetic response.

And last, but not least, we must bridge the gap between Christian academic circles and the rest of the charismatic community. The goal is to instill confidence and promote unity and oneness in the body of Christ. And to realize the important role and responsibility God has given us, as charismatic believers and defenders of the Word of Faith.

Acknowledgements

First, I want thank each and every one of one of my friends and colleagues who were so gracious enough to give their time and assistance for the interviews in this book. Your stories and personal testimonies have contributed more than you will ever know because each one of you is a precious jewel in God's house. Thanks for the confidence you have given me through your kindness and faith in Christ.

Next, I'd like to especially say thank you to Dr. Conny Williams for her vote of confidence through out the entire process of the book. You have provided a wealth of knowledge, resources and assistance. And your spirit and approach to the Christian faith represents the personification of an orthodox charismatic Christian. You are the demonstration of the very message I wish to convey throughout these pages. You have been a blessing to me and my family and thanks for all you've done.

Finally, I wish to say thank you to my lovely wife, Kimberly for her tremendous support and encouragement. Your faith in me means more than I could ever express in one life time. Proverbs says, "He who finds a wife finds a good thing and obtains favor from the Lord." You are the expressed image of these words. Thank you for the "PUSH" you have given me to complete this project. But most of all, thank you for the love we share, and the three wonderful children you have given me. Thank you Justin, Brandon and Christopher for your understanding as I sat at the computer, day after day. Every time you asked, "Dad are you finished yet?" it was an encouragement to me to do just that! I love you and thank you from the bottom of my heart.

Chapter 1

THE CHARISMATIC GENESIS

The decade of the Sixties ushered in the winds of change for just about every area of life and every cultural institution world over. The United States and Russia were then engaged in a race for outer space, when just a few years earlier, men could only dream of such a thing. College campuses became social and political hotbeds as thousands of students erupted in protest and demonstration against an unpopular war. A new genre of music, affectionately known as Rock-n-Roll by youngsters of the day, was forcing its way into mainstream acceptance. It seemed to threaten everything that was called good and wholesome. And right on the heels of its introduction was the arrival of a four-man band from Liverpool,

England, who turned the world upside down with something called, *"Beatlemania"*.

And the ideology behind a simple phrase called "free love", seemed to capture the very essence of the era, as an entire generation questioned and challenged established mores and rebelled against the institution of marriage. Yes indeed, *change* was the word of the day! However, the affects of all this social commotion and upheaval helped to create a spiritual awakening in the lives of people everywhere; black and white, young and old, rich or poor, bond or free. This new spiritual awareness provided the perfect opportunity for the church to minister to a world that was literally looking for The Answer to all of their questions.

Change Agents

It is important to understand that all of this did not occur by random chance. You see, when changes of this magnitude take place in the natural world, it is because of changes that have already begun in the spiritual realm. Such changes, whether good or evil, are always due to supernatural forces behind the scenes that are at war for the souls of men. Light and darkness, good and evil, right and wrong, are in a constant battle to advance the agenda of one kingdom over the other. Jesus instructed His disciples to pray to the Father, ***"Your kingdom come. Your will be done on earth as it is in heaven*** (Matthew

6:10)". And when they prayed He said, ***"And I will give you the keys of the kingdom of heaven, and whatever you bind on earth will be bound in heaven, and whatever you loose on earth will be loosed in heaven"*** (Matthew 16:19). It would appear then as Christians in particular, that we have the power to affect the forces of change upon the world around us.

All throughout the pages of scripture we can find examples of individuals who were instrumental in helping to initiate and facilitate the winds of change. In the second chapter of the gospel of Luke, we have just such a record of two intercessors for change, named Simeon and Anna. Their story begins in the twenty-fifth verse, where it states that Simeon had been waiting on the ***Consolation of Israel,*** and the Holy Spirit was upon him (Luke 2:25). The scripture describes him as ***"a just and devout man."*** Why would the writer of the passage make a point to mention this fact about Simeon? I believe it's because the writer's choice of words give us insight into why God used him. By telling us that Simeon was just, we see that he was justified in the same way that Abraham was justified. And how was he justified? By faith of course! For Abraham believed God, and it was counted unto him, for righteousness (Gen 15:6).

Therefore, Simeon was a man of faith just like Abraham, and his faith was demonstrated in his devotion and faithfulness. Faithfulness and devotion to what you ask? The passage goes on to say, *"...he waited for the fulfillment of the promise of the Consolation of Israel."* So through faith Simeon waited in prayer, anticipation and expectation, to see the promise fulfilled. In verse 26, the Holy Spirit reveals to him that he would not see death until he had seen the Lord's Christ. Luke goes on to tell us that Simeon proclaimed a blessing upon and prophesied about the life of the Christ child.

Then, in the same passage, the scripture mentions Anna. It says that, *"this woman was a widow of about eighty-four years, who did not depart from the temple, but served God with fasting and prayers night and day* (Luke 2:36-38)." Despite her age and personal loss, she continued to intercede, with the expectation of seeing the promise. For which, the scripture says she gave thanks and spoke of Him, *"to all those who looked for the redemption in Jerusalem."*

Simeon and Anna were intercessors and agents for change! They were looking for the new and better Way that God had promised. By faith they were instrumental through intercession and expectation, strategically chosen by God, and placed in the temple at the right time. You may ask, "Well do we have any such record of key individuals who were instrumental in interceding for the birth of the Charismatic movement?" I believe we do have a record of just such an individual, a man by the name of Smith Wigglesworth.

To say the least, Smith Wigglesworth was a man of faith and action. There is plenty of information available about his life and ministry, including period newspaper articles, the sermons he preached, and books written about him. He was born in England in 1859 and came to salvation in Christ at an early age. Wigglesworth was not an exceptionally eloquent speaker by any means, but he believed in the power of God to touch and change lives, and many were won to Christ as a result of his one-on-one evangelistic ministry.

However in 1907, Wigglesworth experienced a sudden and dynamic change in ministry, when he received the baptism of the Holy Spirit. This anointing marked a new beginning in his ministry that brought new boldness and power to preach the uncompromising word of God, with a genuine heart of compassion for the lost. It was also the beginning of God's impartation of grace, to operate in the gift of faith, with an emphasis on miracles and healing. He believed that the manifestation of the gifts of the Spirit were not just for the early church, but for the modern day church as well.

The message of faith was front and center in the life and ministry of Smith Wigglesworth. Reportedly, he often encouraged people to "only believe" and "have faith in God". He believed he had been called by God to deliver the message of faith to the people of God. In fact, Wigglesworth was expecting a new and exciting move of

God. In 1936 during one of his many evangelistic meetings, he prophesied about a time to come, when God would send a revival of the spiritual gifts. He predicted that mainline denominations would begin to embrace the gifts and the people of God would once again operate in the power and anointing of the Holy Spirit[1]. That "move of God", which was specifically mentioned and so accurately foretold by the man of God, has been revealed in our day. It has unmistakably, undeniably and unapologetically become known as the Charismatic Movement!

After forty years in the ministry of evangelistic preaching and healing, Smith Wigglesworth passed away in 1947. Although Wigglesworth did not live to see his prophecy come to pass, he was certainly instrumental in facilitating the winds of change that would ultimately pave the way, for the fulfillment of Gods promise.

Another instrumental individual I came across while doing the research on this subject was a gentleman by the name of Reverend Harald Bredesen. In a tribute article featured on the popular Christian television show the 700 Club, Reverend Bredesen was referred to as the first modern charismatic minister.[2] From the article, Harald is quoted as having received the baptism of the Holy Spirit in 1946. I believe Wigglesworth's prediction about a mainline denominational embrace of the charismatic gifts began it's fruition through the ministry of Harald Bredesen.

In fact, in a letter to the editor of Eternity Magazine, Harald Bredesen and Jean Stone Williams coined the term "Charismatic Renewal."[3] Also in Encyclopedia Britannica's first expose´ on the Charismatic movement featured a photograph of Reverend Bredesen. And according to the Evangelical Dictionary, Reverend Harald Bredesen is referred to as the father of the modern charismatic movement. This is very interesting to me considering the fact that Smith Wigglesworth passed away one year after Bredesen received the baptism of the Holy Spirit. It was as if God shifted the charismatic flame of faith like a torch from one man to another.

As a Lutheran minister, Bredesen became the first clergyman from a mainline denomination to receive the Pentecostal experience of the baptism of the Holy Spirit. Harald said that he was unique because there was not another church pastor who had received the baptism of the Holy Spirit and remained in the historic Lutheran Church. According to Bredesen, he offered to surrender his ordination and credentials, but to their credit, the Lutheran Church rejected his offer and asked him to continue in Lutheran ministry.

Bredesen was certainly a man called by God to be one of the most influential change agents of our time. After graduating from seminary, Harald went to work for the World Council of Churches as the Public Relations Secretary for the World Council of Christian Education. However, he wasn't just a minister of the gospel, but he was also a mentor, a facilitator and a talented writer. His list of accomplishments included the founding of his Prince of Peace Foundation, which granted recognition awards to other remarkable Christian leaders like Mother Teresa in 1989 and Billy Graham in 2004. The Prince of Peace Prize was also awarded to influential political leaders like Egyptian President Anwar Sadat in 1980 and posthumously to King Hussein of Jordan (received by his son King Abdullah) in 1999.

Harald Bredesen had a very special ministry to world leaders. The relationships and friendships he formed included world leaders like Presidents Jimmy Carter and Ronald Reagan, Menachem Begin, and Anwar Sadat. Again, in the article, Pat Robertson mentions the fact that "He and Anwar Sadat, for example, developed a great personal friendship when he interviewed him in Egypt." Robertson called Bredesen's ministry to world leaders "legendary." The most interesting aspect about this man of God is not his list of accomplishments, but rather the way in which he impacted the lives of others around him. The authors of the 700 Club article are clear in their intent and purpose, as they point out, "...most of all, Harold will be remembered by so many as a wonderful friend." His son, David Bredesen is quoted as having said of Harald, "There's so many people that have been affected by him: ministers, musicians, world leaders, all kinds of people. They all have been touched by Dad. But he didn't touch them for his gain; he touched them for God's word."

According to a press release dated December 29, 2006[4], Harald Bredesen passed away at the age of 88 years old. Although he is no longer with us, the ripple affects of this modern day example of an anointed ambassador for change are still being felt throughout entire Church. His influence was not limited to the landscape of Christendom, but he touched and impacted the political powers that govern the world around us. How did Bredesen do so much in so little time? It is because he was known as a man of prayer. And through prayer, he was able to change the world! As Pat Robertson noted about his friend and mentor, "God broke the mold. There'll never be another on like Harald. We honor him. We bless him, and I miss his laughter."

Bredesen and Wigglesworth represent just two examples of the many individuals God used as change agents prior to the 1967 outpour. There were many more men and women who received the baptism of the Holy Spirit, then answered the call of God to influence the Church and impact the world through charismatic ministry. Men such as William Branham, Gordon Lindsay, Oral Roberts and T.L. Osborn were all early pioneers of the Charismatic Renewal. Others include common individuals like John and Joan Baker, an Episcopalian couple who received the baptism of the Holy Ghost back in 1959. Together with Episcopalian minister Dennis Bennett, who publically announced to his traditional congregation that he had received the baptism of the Holy Spirit, became change agents in the California Episcopal community of their day. Each of these individuals represents a "Simeon" or an "Anna." The kind of people God used as instruments to prepare the way and initiate change for our day.

GOD Initiates Change

Throughout church history, whenever the people of God would stir-up the winds of change by prayer for renewal and revival in the Spirit, God then caused those winds to blow down upon this natural world to affect human events. We can see a perfect example of this principle given in the Old Testament book of Joel, where we read the account of a disaster that strikes the kingdom of Judah. The people of God had experienced devastation and ruin, because of judgment for their sins, so God sent a man to give them a message. It was a sobering message that was first directed to the elders and priests of Judah, then to the inhabitants of the land (Joel 1:13, 14 & 2:12, 13). The Lord said if they would simply turn to Him in repentance, with fasting and prayer with weeping, He would not only be merciful and relent, but also leave a blessing behind (Joel 2:14).

The Lord goes on to make a prophetic promise of hope and restoration to His people. He said, *"I will restore to you the years the locust has eaten... You shall eat in plenty and be satisfied, and praise the name of the Lord your God, Who has dealt wondrously with you. And it shall come to pass afterward that I will pour out My spirit on all flesh; your sons and daughters shall prophesy, your old men shall dream dreams, your young men shall see visions and I will pour out My Spirit on your maidservants in those days* (Joel 2:25-29)." This promise was initially fulfilled on the Day of Pentecost and continues as an ongoing fulfillment throughout the church age.

The Reformation is one example of just such an outpouring of the Spirit of God. As true Christians prayed for change and deliverance, God sent men such as Martin Luther, and later John Wesley, to confront the church and promote repentance. In the very same manner, the period of change in the sixties began because of prayer for spiritual renewal and revival, around the turn of the century. It can be traced back to events such as the Azusa Street Revival of 1906, lead by William J. Seymour, where God poured out His spirit upon a group that met for prayer in a small church in Los Angeles, California. What began as a prayer meeting later became a revival meeting that lasted about three years. Many souls were saved and lives changed as God revealed Himself to an entire community through miracles, signs and wonders.

We should also consider the many untold accounts of civil rights injustices endured by African Americans and the struggles that were carried to God in prayer. Prayers of intercession and painful travail, covered in blood, sweat and tears that helped to birth and support the civil rights movement of the early sixties. Again God raised up a man with a message, the late Dr. Martin Luther King, who's divinely inspired dream was to bring repentance and healing for his nation. Time and time again, it has been the same message of repentance and restoration, which our loving God continues to extend today.

Something worth noting is that the Charismatic Dictionary identifies the year 1967 as the beginning of the Charismatic movement[5]. Although some may argue the point, the 1967 outpour of the Spirit God marked a return and renewal of the gifts of the Spirit to the body of Christ. That is not to diminish the importance of the work and movements of GOD prior to 1967. On the contrary, it was simply the end-time fulfillment of the prophecy spoken of by the prophet Joel, and initially delivered to the church of the Apostles in the book of Acts. The revival of which was seen by a man God used as the Apostle of Faith, who spoke about just such a time, when the charismatic gifts of the Spirit would again operate in the Church. Finally, it brought forth the birth of a new member in the Christian community; the charismatic community of faith, whose influence upon body of Christ is indelible and undeniable.

Considering the fact that the prophecy in Joel certainly included the Jewish nation to whom it was written, one of the most interesting aspects about these events is the time period in which they occurred. The possibility of its application to the Jews seemed unlikely prior to Israel becoming a nation in 1948. Later, the Six Day War took place in June 1967, when Israel took control of the Promised Land. The event represented a major change in the history and the future of the Israeli nation. It was an important and necessary component for the fulfillment of the prophecy. I believe that it is clear that God was orchestrating these events to correspond with events and outpour of the Charismatic Renewal. With all of the changes that took place during the latter part of that decade, there is no question that we needed a significant outpour of God's grace and power during that tumultuous time. His impartation of grace helped to change the landscape of the people of Israel and the Church at large.

Resistance to Change

As the decade of the Sixties ended, God began to pour out His spirit on all those who were sincerely seeking to know the truth about who He is and how to find Him, just as He had promised. Young people in particular were coming to know Jesus, getting saved and turning to the church. Like babes, they desired to hear the sincere milk of the Word, from ministers who would share with them the truth of God's word. I have heard many people tell of how they came to faith in some of the most unorthodox places and unconventional methods.

From the urban inner cities of New York to the beaches of the California coast, folks were coming to faith in Christ, receiving the gift of salvation, and being baptized in the Holy Spirit on street corners and college campuses everywhere. I've even heard of one account about an individual who came to on a parking lot in the back of a VW mini bus! However, this move of God would prove to be a challenge for the tradition church, because of its resistance to change. You see, these were the same young people who were considered to be long hair, bare footed, trouble-making hippies prior to their conversion. And now they were coming into the orthodox churches with all of their questions, ideals and convictions.

I believe this is where many local churches of the day failed to pass the test. It was a test of love and acceptance, and an opportunity to demonstrate the kind of love that Christ had for the church, as He gave Himself for us. Just like the church of Martin Luther's day, they forgot that Christ died for the sins of common men and women. Some pastors were even unwilling to let young converts enter into worship services, unless they were properly dressed. Thankfully, this was no the case in every scenario. I've heard many stories about pastors and preachers who refused to be blinded by judgmental discrimination and religious traditions of men. They chose rather to look beyond the outward appearance, into the born again heart of the individuals, who were seeking to know the truth.

One case in point that comes to mind, is from the personal testimony of a minister who is a pastor of a well know church, in the California area. I heard him on the radio one evening, while driving home from work, as he shared about his experience as a new believer. In the account, he told the story of how he was rejected by various pastors and churches because of his appearance, which he described as the look of the typical teenager of that era. He mentioned that he had long hair back in the day (as he made light of being one of the "bald guys" now) and that he and his friends dressed in little more than a T-shirt and blue jeans. He went on to express his deep appreciation and admiration for the one pastor who did welcome him in.

The minister went on to end his testimony by saying that had it not been for the love and patience of that compassionate, southern California pastor, he himself would not have become a pastor at all. I thank God for such men of faith! Such individuals are sensitive to the gentle wind of the Holy Spirit and will not to resist the loving direction of the Spirit. They choose rather to be intercessors for the body of Christ, and facilitators of Gods plan for His church, and the world. The testimony of this southern California pastor is a perfect example of the kind of people God began to raise up out of those changing times. Many of the young men and women of that era were considered hippies, beach bums, and peace disturbers by the political, social and religious establishment of the day. But these were exactly the kind of people God was changing and choosing to carry the message of a new movement.

As the church entered the new decade of the 1970's, God began to pour out His Spirit upon college campuses all across America. Out of those campuses the Lord raised up agents of change for a new era in church history. As God poured out His spirit upon the hearts and lives of young people who were sold out for Jesus, they began to create new ways to worship and serve. New and exciting ministries were born out of a desire to reach the world for Christ through love, music and evangelism. With a fresh evangelistic anointing, ministries such as Campus Crusade for Christ, Evangelism Explosion and Jews for Jesus were at the forefront of evangelistic outreach efforts of the day. As the collective efforts of those ministries began to grow in size and influence, another movement was born that affectionately and appropriately became known as the Jesus Movement.

Chapter 2

JUST SAY NONDENOMINATIONAL

Origins of Denominationalism

For the purpose of clarity, let's begin by establishing a good foundation for understanding what is meant by the term denomination. According to Merriam-Webster's Dictionary[6], denomination is defined as "4: a religious organization whose congregations are united in their adherence to its beliefs and practices." Therefore, denominationalism is defined as "1: devotion to denominational principles or interests 2: the emphasizing of denominational differences to the point of being narrowly exclusive: sectarianism." According to Wikipedia[7], denominationalism is defined as "the division of a religion into separate religious denominations. The term is particularly used in reference to the various Protestant schools of thought." By all accounts, the religious applications of this word were born out of necessity to address and facilitate the results of the Protestant Reformation.

Origins of the idea of denominationalism date back to the 1700's when Parliament called the Westminster Assembly together to establish the theological and liturgical direction of the Church of England. At the time, the major religious groups represented were the Church of Rome, the Church of England and Scottish Kirk. Over the course of the meetings, the independents were the most avid supporters of the notion that the true church could not be confined to any particular ecclesiastical institution. The results of the discourse led to the Westminster Confession of Faith. It reflected the influence of the independent representatives, and hinted at the idea of denominationalism.

Within the confession is the basic notion that several churches, despite disunity, were part of the true universal Church. Prior to this event, sectarian religious groups were considered dissenters from the faith. That new understanding of the Church helped to create the framework for the construct used throughout the twentieth century to understand Protestantism. This view of Protestantism influenced the British colonies that came to North America. In fact, early American Protestantism was largely comprised of groups considered to be religious dissenters by the established Church of England. Therefore, the early American churches decided against the establishment of a single state recognized church or religion. Instead, they agreed to recognize the diversity of each individual religious group, and to accept them as equal members of the universal Church. From this perspective, the term denominationalism was used to reflect the positive expression of religious freedom held within the United States of America.

At the dawn of the twentieth century, sociologist Max Weber was one of the first sociologists in religion to identify and develop the dichotomy between church and sect. However, the term was popularized by a student of Weber named Ernst Troeltsch. Troeltsch wrote a book entitled *The Social Teaching of the Christian Churches.*[8] This book popularized the term for many Protestants in the United States. He used the concept of denominationalism more narrowly than Weber's distinction of church verses sect.

From the late nineteenth century until the 1960's, a new understanding of denominationalism began to emerge. The term denomination lost its association with religious dissent and functioned as a form of ecclesiastical establishment. Books such as Samuel McCrea Cavert's *The American Churches in the Ecumenical Movement, 1900- 1968* (1968)[9] again helped to redefine the definition of denominationalism. In this book, Samuel Cavert asserts that competition among churches was related to the divisions caused by race and class. It became an instrumental tool that provided a unifying perspective for commentaries written by religious historians to address the Ecumenical Protestant Movement. Such perspectives helped to shape the ecumenical spirit of the emerging Charismatic Movement of the late 1960's and early 1970's.

By the mid-seventies, those within the Charismatic Movement had coined a new phrase intended to describe their position regarding denominational affiliation. When someone asked, "To what denomination do you belong?" The charismatic response became, "I am nondenominational." Usually the person who made the inquiry stood with a look upon their face, as if to say, "And what does that mean?" To which the charismatic Christian would respond with an explanation something like, "That means that I'm not Baptist or Lutheran, nor Catholic, Methodist or Pentecostal. I'm simply a member of the Body of Christ and God's universal Church!"

The term "nondenominational" was an attempt to disassociate charismatic Christians from many of the stigmas, negative connotations and stereotypical ideas associated with denominational affiliations. Things such as clergy titles and religious formalities associated with some traditional, mainstream denominational churches were rejected. Therefore, many who were called to be licensed and/or ordained ministers simply chose to be known as, "Brother John Doe" or "Sister Suzie Christian", rather than "The Reverend, Doctor Jim Highbrow." This choice of attitude came from a desire to distance themselves from the arrogance and false humility associated with such titles and to demonstrate a genuine spirit of humility. It was also an effort to recognize the fact that every true born again believer is equal and important in God's economy! "We then, *as workers together with Him*," became the scriptural basis for common ground in ministry (2Corinthians 6:1).

It was an attitude, which promoted and provided a freedom from the formalities of public worship services and gatherings (like prayer meetings and bible studies). Even Sunday morning worship services had a more casual atmosphere, which allowed Christians to worship with greater freedom of expression when praising God, and even permitted them to come without fear of being rejected because of what they wore to church.

This casual atmosphere also created a format that allowed preachers and teachers to become more intimate in their presentation of the Word. They began to come out from behind the podiums and out of the pulpits, to the areas and spaces right down in front of the pews and seating arrangements. This helped Word of

Faith ministers to connect with their congregations in a way that encouraged a more personal, creative and engaging exposition from the Word. In contrast, such a presentation was unfamiliar to folks who were accustomed to the rigid and impersonal style, found in more traditional church services.

For the most part, the men and women who initially began in the movement were simply trying to get more of God, more of Jesus and more of the Word. Through faith and prayer, they hoped to create an atmosphere where the Holy Spirit could have free course in the ministry of the Word and manifestation of the gifts of the Spirit. And a place where Christians could worship freely, without regard to status, race, religious tradition, or worship style. But unbeknownst to the many individuals involved, who communicated and contributed to the elements that went into creating a basis for nondenominational worship, they also defined the model that would ultimately be used to create the template used for charismatic churches around the globe.

Nondenominational to Interdenominational

To help us get a better understanding of the impact of nondenominational philosophy, let's consider a conversation I had with a teacher and colleague in ministry. Her name is Dr. Conny Williams. She is the dean of a local Bible College, whom I will introduce at length later on in our discussions. In fact, I wanted to interview her because of the wealth of knowledge and experience she has gleaned, from dealing with pastors and laypeople on a first-hand basis. We discussed the ecumenical role and charismatic ministry of the local Bible College she manages. Some of the comments she made about the ministry of her college, and the relationships that she has formed with the students, will help to shed some light on this subject.

Dr. Conny said, "In my opinion, I do not see our college as nondenominational, I believe it is interdenominational." Pastor Conny says that she considers it to be interdenominational because the student body is comprised of people from many different denominations. While naming each digit from one hand to the next, she explained, "We have Baptist people, C.O.G.I.C. people, non-denominational people, former Jehovah witnesses, Methodist, Lutherans and Catholics who attend, just to name a few." However, she also said that she doesn't see this trend as a "direction, or movement" for the church, but rather believes that it is simply a better description of what had been labeled as "non-denominational." As the pastors and laymen of the college work together to support each other's denominational ministry, there is a natural "dynamic cross-affiliation" that takes place.

Pastor Conny contends that this has always been a part of the charismatic experience, "Because when charismatic people open their mouth, you can tell what denomination they came out of." Again, this would account for the blending and meshing of charismatic and traditional aspects of Christianity. However, it is the spirit of this cross-affiliation that I believe is the key to understanding the very same dynamic that is taking place on a larger scale within Christendom. In the first Great Awakening, Thomas Whitfield pushed aside denominational differences with the statement, "Denominations don't get into heaven. Christians do!" It is in this same spirit that those who began the charismatic movement sought to free themselves and others from the bondage of divisive, denominational thinking. I believe it is that same "Spirit of Unity" that has inspired the Ecumenical movement of the last decade or two.

Please understand that I am not talking about those within the ecumenical movement which subscribe to the notion that Christians, Muslims, Buddhists and members of every other religion should unite as one because we serve the same God. Those who hold this ecumenical view point have fallen prey to error and misconception. However, that desire for ecumenical unity that has begun to build bridges and to tear down the barriers which separate the body of Christ is a genuine move of the Holy Spirit.

While I am not aware of anyone within the charismatic community who claimed that the charismatic influence had anything to do with this process, there were however plenty of evangelical proponents that attribute the source of the ecumenical movement to charismatic beginnings. Despite the objections of many evangelical apologetic zealots, God will have His way in the church and the earth. It is clear from scripture that Jesus prayed that His body would one day be made one. Because God will most certainly honor and fulfill every petition made by His Son, you can be sure that what Jesus prayed will come to pass.

Whether it started because of charismatic influence matters not! It's true origin and source of power is the Holy Spirit of God. Since the Holy Spirit is at work in the Church to bring about the fulfillment of unity and oneness in the body of Christ, as members in particular of the charismatic community, we certainly want to be a part of that work. Therefore, any influence that we may have upon the process; we joyfully do so in the spirit of unity.

Chapter 3
FREE FROM TRADITION

Over the years, I have heard lots of reasons why people began to leave the security of their denominational affiliation, for the new charismatic phenomenon. But most can be categorized under four particular reoccurring themes that surface with each story that I have heard from individuals, who joined a Word of Faith/Charismatic Church. If you have come from a traditional denominational background, you too may identify with one or more of the following reasons.

• The individual left seeking better teaching and a greater understanding of the word of God to satisfy the need for growth and maturity.

- The individual left in search of freedom from oppressive traditional standards and/or pharisaical religious legalism.

- The individual left in search of truth because of erroneous teaching propagated by their denominational affiliation.

- The individual left to follow after the supernatural charismatic manifestation of the gifts (miracle, signs and wonders).

In Search of Food for Growth

The first of these issues is in fact the most common reason cited by many people I know, as they discussed what prompted them to leave their former denominational affiliation. Case in point, there is the testimony of Mrs. Virginia Martin. Virginia and her husband Laurence (L.C.) have been long time friends and colleagues in the faith. She has served as an educator and school counselor in the St. Louis Public School System for almost thirty years. She is also the founder and president of Caring and Sharing Women's Ministry and currently serves as an associate minister at a local nondenominational charismatic church.

One Sunday after service, I asked if we could talk about her experiences in the charismatic movement, as well as any thought she may have about the subject. She agreed and invited my wife and me over after church. After settling in at the kitchen table of her home, we began our interview, as she told the testimony of how she came to faith in Christ; and subsequently, how she was introduced to the Word of Faith/Charismatic movement. She explained that as a teenager growing up, she and her mother attended a large Baptist church. As we began the initial questions of the interview, I asked Virginia what single experience or incident caused her to leave her traditional denominational upbringing in favor of attending a charismatic church. In response, she said, "It wasn't 'a single incident.' It was a lack of teaching in one area that made me leave the church."

I then asked Minister Virginia to elaborate on her response. She continued by saying, "In addition to the dissension in the body, there was some teaching that was not done. And that was because, not that the church had changed, but it was because I was changing." I then asked how she had changed. She replied, "As a result of my, umm ... (as she paused for thought), I had received the baptism of the Holy Spirit. And so I went to the pastor and asked why he didn't teach on it; and he did believe in the Holy Spirit, with the evidence of speaking in tongues. And he told me that you have to give milk to babes. He said that was the reason why the teaching didn't go any deeper than it did. Because of the congregational majority, he had to teach to the majority.

Now my argument to that was, 'If you don't begin to teach them more, how will they ever get to the place where they don't just need milk?' And they can only take milk. Milk is fine! In fact, a good glass of milk with your meat is good. That's my thought now! But back then, all I knew that if you want give me more, then how can I grow. And how can they grow (the congregation) if they don't get anymore. So his answer wasn't satisfactory." In conclusion, Virginia said that it still took another two or three years before she actually left, because of heart ties to family and friends in the church. But eventually she had to leave after her exposure to the in-depth teaching she found in a circle of charismatic Christian friends. She left to satisfy the need to growth in her knowledge and understanding of the word of God.

To her point, I asked her to explain just how she became exposed to the Word of Faith message and the charismatic community. She explained that while attending college, a few of the students used to get together for Bible study. Among that group of friends was a gentleman by the name of Gerald Deveron Ford. According to Minister Virginia's testimony, "Gerald's teaching was the teachings of Kenneth Hagan, Kenneth Copeland. And he sat under them; he put himself under their teaching. And so what he learned he taught us. And once he started teaching us and recommending other people, then we would listen to those people also. So that's basically how it happened."

As fate would have it, Pastor Gerald Ford was not only instrumental in bringing the Word of Faith message to that small group of college students, but he also went on to start one of the first charismatic churches in the St. Louis African American community. I too had the opportunity to know him and to experience his unique style of preaching and teaching. Although he has since pasted away, he is remembered by those who knew him as an exceptional teacher of God's Word.

In Search of Freedom from Oppression

One of the best examples of this scenario came from the testimony of Dr. Conny Williams. Dr. Conny told me that she received her salvation after attending a service at a little Church of God in Christ, in Centralia, Illinois, back in 1985. During my interview with Dr. Conny, I asked her why she left her former C.O.G.I.C. affiliation. She said without a doubt, it was because of the freedom that came through the teaching of the word.

As she elaborated upon her response, she said, "I have learned that the word of God frees me! Because you see, in the traditional church, we didn't learn that. We didn't know that! All we heard was don't do, do this, don't that and "You're going to hell!" People were going to hell every Sunday and 'getting saved' every Sunday. And the Charismatic movement moved in and said, "Hey…your salvation is secure. You are saved. God is excited about you!"

That's the kind of "good news" that God wanted to convey to believers in the body of Christ. This was part of the divine message and purpose of the Charismatic movement in its beginning. The explosion of the gift of teaching brought an understanding of the message of God's love and acceptance for those who would receive Him. It also taught us how to live a life of salvation through the power of the Holy Spirit. That kind of teaching became absolutely vital for those who were in need of a loving Savior.

In Search of Truth vs. Propaganda

As we address the next reason cited by some people who left their former denominational affiliation, I thought perhaps this issue may best be illustrated by sharing my own personal testimony as a young teen in search of the truth. I was sixteen years old at the time and very active within the church, but everything changed after a conversation I had with the pastor of our congregation. It was one of those conversations that completely turns your whole world upside down, and hurts so much that it causes you to grow up a little sooner than you'd like. I mentioned earlier that it was at about this age that I first attended a Word of Faith bible study. That experience left me charged and eager to get into my own personal study of the topics and principles that were discussed on that evening. After a while, I began to bring up the various questions and topics, from the fellowship Bible study, during studies at my own local church for discussion.

On one particular occasion, the issue of sanctification came up, and a discussion ensued about how Christians are set apart from the world became the topic of the study for the evening. And of course, "yours truly" with all of my many questions, decided to make a note regarding a statement made by the teacher of the charismatic bible study that went something like this. "God isn't concerned about how you dress, or what you look like, or the way you comb your hair! What He wants to see is that our hearts and lives have been changed from the inside out."

Immediately following his statements, a young woman asked a question in a most uncertain tone. "So you're saying God doesn't care if I wear pants to church?" To which the teacher responded, "No, He doesn't! He said...Wait!" as he quickly flipped the pages of his Bible to find the passage that came to mind. "Let's go to 1Samuel 16:7. See, it say, 'Man looks at the outward appearance,' but God looks at and judges the heart!" All of a sudden, all kinds of bells, whistles, stop signs and red flags began to go off in my head, because at my church, it was an outright sin for a woman to wear pants!

Needless to say, I could hardly wait to get back to my church to see what the saints in my Pentecostal bible study group would say about the issue. But first, I wanted to know for myself, what the Bible had to say. The new Bible study had taught me how to use reference materials, other translations, and commentary and study skills. So, I studied and searched for every scripture I could find that seemed to relate to that topic.

Finally, I was ready to approach my Pentecostal study group to ask for help in understanding the apparent contradiction in teaching, from the other study group. I simply asked, "Can a woman wear pants and still be saved?" And man! You'd a thought I had just started world war three, with all the conversation and commotion that ensued for the next half hour! When the dust finally settled, I still hadn't received a satisfactory answer that was soundly supported by scripture. Therefore, I was told that I should talk to the pastor and that he could straighten out my thinking regarding the matter, so I asked for an audience with my pastor. A couple of weeks went by and I began to reconsider, because I was just plain scared, but the day had arrived and it was too late to change my mind. After service on a Sunday afternoon, the pastor asked if could stay over for a few minutes to discuss my concerns. I agreed and we sat down on the front row of the sanctuary pews to begin our discussion. "So tell me," he said, "what's all the fuss about you and this issue of women and salvation?" I could hardly respond as my throat seemed to instantly dry out and my heart raced as if it would pound right out of my shirt!

Well, we began to talk and the more we talked, the more heated the discussion became. He presented each point of defense for the position of the church and I countered with information I had received through my studies. For every reason he gave me, I could only respond with a like, "Well why does the Bible say this?" as I scurried to find chapter and verse, and to open my notes for him to see. I remember thinking, "God please...please forgive me for arguing with the man of God like this! Lord, have mercy, please!"

Finally, after about an hour of debating the issue, something happened that I never expected. As we sat there, quiet and frustrated, my pastor turned to look me square in the eye, then exhaled and said, "Tim, you are right! A woman's salvation has nothing to do with what she can or cannot wear. But I can't preach that because I would loose my congregation." At that very moment, something happened on the inside of me that's hard to explain. It was as if something dropped and made a sick, sinking feeling in the heart of that sixteen-year old boy.

The pastor went on to say that if I could not understand that, then maybe it was time for me to move my membership elsewhere. So after thanking him for his time and honesty, we ended the discussion and needless to say, I moved my membership a few months later. I should stop right here for a moment, just to say that I really appreciate how my pastor really took out the time to even listen to what I had to say. All young Christians should be so blessed to have a shepherd who cared as much about the sheep of God! He is no longer here in the land of the living, but I'm certain that he is among the saints of God in heaven.

In retrospect, I suppose the most interesting aspect of the whole experience is that my former pastor was exactly right. At the time, moving my membership to a charismatic church was the best thing I could have done, because it caused me to grow and mature spiritually in ways I could have never imagined.

In Search of Miracles, Signs and Wonders

The fourth and final reason that many people left the stability of their former church is certainly the least justifiable of all. To their shame, and to ours as a community of faith, many individuals left in search of miracles and to follow after signs and wonders. Of course this was nothing new. Even in the days of the ministry of Jesus, there were those among the crowd that came not to hear the words He spoke, but to see the next miracle He would perform. We find one such account in John 6:1-35, beginning at verse two we read, *"Then a great multitude followed Him, because they saw His signs which He performed on those who were diseased."*

After a careful analysis of the text, we find three groups of people scattered among the multitude. The first group is those seeking miracles of healing for physical illness. Notice that Jesus does not send them away. He instead is moved with compassion and begins to meet the physical and spiritual needs of everyone within the multitude. However, in order to meet their natural need for food, Jesus chooses to perform a miracle.

Within this passage, we find legitimate reasons for those who seek the miraculous signs and wonders of God. It is to seek His hand of intervention for our lives to meet legitimate needs that are impossible for us to meet ourselves. Sometimes as an act of faith we have to go where the spirit of God is moving. Therefore, individuals who may have traveled a great distance, or gone to another church to attend a charismatic worship service, are well with in the will of God and the teaching of scripture to do so. I have known many people that left the traditional church they attended, in hopes of finding a charismatic service where the gift of healing was in operation.

Now Jesus, being the great teacher and communicator that He is, also chose to use this opportunity as a teachable moment for the disciples. In verses 3 through 10, we are introduced to the second reason for the miracle of feeding the five thousand. Therefore, the second group people we find amid the multitude is individuals being taught by Jesus. He uses the miracle as an object lesson for His disciples. As a point of education and examination for the students who followed Him, Jesus asked Philip, *"Where shall we buy bread that these may eat?"* And Philip answered in the exact manner that Jesus knew he would; with a response that was not based upon faith, but rather upon the limited resources of human ability. However, Jesus does find a spark of faith in the response of another disciple named Andrew. Andrew declares, *"There is a lad here who has five barley loaves and two small fish, but what are they among so many?"* Notice that the resources don't even belong to Andrew, yet he discovers the Answer to his question in his obedience to the instructions of Christ.

The third group of sign seekers we see among the crowd is men seeking signs and wonders for the sake of misdirected interest in His power and glory. In verses 14 and 15, we discover their true motive. The text says, *"Then those men, when they had seen the sign that Jesus did, said, 'This is truly the Prophet who is to come into the world. Therefore when Jesus perceived that they were about to come and take Him by force to make Him king, He departed again to the mountain by Himself alone."* They sought to use God's glory for their own personal gain.

Later on after they discovered that Jesus and His disciples had departed, the Bible says that they too *"got into boats and came to Capernaum, seeking Jesus."* Once they arrived on the other side of the sea, they found Jesus and asked, *"Rabbi, when did you come here?"* It is at this point in verse 26 that Jesus deals with the motive of those who seek after Him for the miraculous exploits. He then explains that they have missed the very reason for the miracles He performed. He says to them, *"Most assuredly I say to you, you seek Me not because you saw the signs, but because you ate of the loaves and were filled."* It is clear that they are only interested in the sheer spectacle of what Jesus can do and how they might benefit from it.

Over the course of the next few verses, Jesus tells the crowd in no uncertain terms that the signs and wonders that they seek are intended to lead them to the truth about the person and power of Christ. Therefore He instructs them not to be so preoccupied with efforts that only minister to their physical needs, but rather to work

45

"for the food which endures to everlasting life, which the Son of Man will give you." They inquired again about the miracles as they asked, *"What shall we do that we may work the works of God?"* And again Jesus redirected their attention away from the miraculous, and back to purpose for the miracles. He says once again, *"This is the work of God that you believe in Him whom He sent."*

Finally, they expose the misguided intent of their heart, as they asked the wrong questions of Jesus for the third time. They asked, *"What sign will you perform then, that we may see it and believe in You? What work will you do?"* In reference to signs and wonders, they cite another time in Jewish history when God performed miracles to make provision for His people. *"Our fathers ate the manna in the desert; as it is written, 'He gave them bread from heaven to eat.'"* Once again Jesus presents a challenge to their understanding of who performed the miracle of provision and the purpose for which it was performed. Jesus plainly tells them that Moses was not responsible for the miracle of manna from heaven, but God was the source behind the supernatural event. Jesus then reiterates the fact that the miraculous sign of bread from heaven was intended to point to the true Bread of Heaven. In John 6:35 Jesus says, *"I am the bread of life."*

Wisdom for the Miraculous

Ok! Now that we have established some of the legitimate reasons people follow miracles, and the purpose for signs and wonders, it is time to discuss some of the negative aspects of our affection for this area of faith. In an effort to achieve balance and wisdom in this area, we must acknowledge the fact that far too many charismatic Christians are so enamored by the supernatural of faith that they loose sight of the necessity for wisdom and discernment. Far too many Christians go from church to church, city to city and town to town looking for the next big move of God. Such individuals are like spiritual junkies looking for the next supernatural high, but as soon as the show is over and the truth of the teaching gets hard to bear, then they are off and running again in search of another supernatural high.

As I penned these words, I realized that they were not my own, but I had heard them spoken before by someone else. His name is Pastor Femi Omotayo, pastor of Jesus House Church. Pastor Femi is originally from Nigeria where he attended college and graduated with a B.A. degree in Philosophy and has served as a pastor since 1995. I had the opportunity to visit Pastor Femi's church on several occasions and had heard his admonitions to the congregation to endeavor to be balanced Christians regarding the subject of signs and wonders. So I wanted to talk with him about his perspective on the charismatic movement. When I contacted Pastor Femi about an interview, he seemed happy to oblige, but was concerned about the distance of the drive from my house to his. After I assured him that I did not mind making the forty-five minute trip for an opportunity to speak with him, we set the date and I was on my way.

When I finally arrived at Pastor Femi's home, I found him at work in the back yard of his beautiful home. He was busy laying a decorative stone pad to compliment the large deck that he had built. During our conversation on the phone, he asked if I would wear something comfortable to work in, so I came prepared to help. We had a great time getting to know each other, talking about ministry and the Word, and doing guy-stuff. You know…the kind of project that you can stand back and take pride in after you're finished. And when we were done, that's exactly what we did. The pad turned out great! Femi could hardly wait to move his bar-b-que grill from its place on the deck to its new home on the freshly laid stone platform. When Mrs. Omotayo stepped outside to see the finished product, Pastor Femi was rewarded with a big smile and a nod of approval. After which, we went inside to cool off and rest after a job well done. As Mrs. Omotayo served us up a nice cold glass of lemonade, we sat down, I took out my tape recorder, and we began the interview.

After the preliminary introduction, I jumped right into this subject by reminding Pastor Femi of his comments about people who seek after signs and wonders. He responded with affirmation as he recalled the reasons for his comments on the subject. He began by saying, "The Bible says that miracles are a witness to the Word, but they are not the only witness to the Word; we have the inner witness of the Holy Spirit. Miracles are supposed to convince people of the truth. That's their job, to confirm the truth. So the miracles are not supposed to stand alone; they are supposed to work with the truth. But then God is sovereign. God can decide, 'You know what? For this particular person, to convince him of the truth, I need to do a demonstration of the supernatural, to convince him that the word he hears is truth. God may decide that he doesn't need that; what he needs is the Holy Spirit speaking to his heart. So then the frequency of it, or the absence of it, is dependent on the move of the Holy Spirit at that time."

Without missing a beat, Pastor Femi continued to say, "Although the Bible promises us everything; healing, deliverance and all of those things, they are basically God intervening in the course of nature. So since the earth has been judged, the earth is corrupt; it is decaying and dying and part of that is sickness and disease. Now when God intervenes in the course of the decay and corruption, of course what you have is (the miracle of) healing."

Now there are some folks who are so rapped up in them (in miracles), because they are spectacular. Yes, they are exciting, but in reality the Bible says that even the devil can counterfeit miracles. 2 Thessalonians 2: 9, 10 says, *"The coming of the one is according to the working of Satan, with all power, signs and lying wonders, and with all unrighteous deception among those who perish, because they did not receive the love of the truth, that they might be saved."*

What you have are those people who end up being very superficial. You know…they are like drug addicts who need a new high. They need something every now and then to pep them up. Well the Bible says 'that the just shall live by faith,' and it says 'as many who are led by the Spirit of God,' they are the sons of God; not as many who are led by miracles, or as many who are led by their feelings. So at the end of the day, we have to be careful not to forget that it starts with faith, in the middle it is faith, and at the end it is faith.

✝
Chapter Four
A GIFT TO THE BODY

In an effort to increase our understanding of the positive influence and overall impact the Word of Faith movement has had upon the church, and to build a foundation for an appreciation of the manifold ways in which the charismatic community has ministered to the body of Christ, I thought it might help if we take a look at some of those contributions. To this end, let us consider the following topics as gifts to the body of Christ.

"A New Song"

Arguably, one of the greatest gifts and most appreciated blessings given to the modern day church was delivered via the gift of music. It began in the hearts and minds of a few individuals, born out of a desire to worship in a more simple and intimate way. And God, in His magnificent and wonderful way, took a spark that began in the heart of a few individuals and ignited a firestorm the spread across every continent on the globe. He took that idea (the desire to worship in a more simple and intimate way) and used it to create an entirely new genre of music that would impact a generation and would affectionately become known as Contemporary Praise and Worship.

I must say that in my own life, as a musician, songwriter and a worship leader, music has been an indispensable part of my Christian experience. From the age of nine years old, I believe that God began to prepare me for a life of worship through music. In fact, when my parent asked what I wanted for my ninth birthday, my response was adamant as I told them that I wanted a guitar for my birthday that year! Well, to my surprise, it wasn't my parents who took me seriously, but rather it was my grandmother who purchased a brand new acoustic guitar and gave it to me as a gift. Needless to say, she was the best grandmother anyone could have, and her gift of love served as a springboard, which catapulted my life into a new direction. Later that same year, just after my conversion experience, I gave my life to Christ and began to sing in the "young people's choir" at church. And to this day, I still have very fond memories of that experience.

By the time I was fifteen, I had already begun to play guitar in church and where ever the choir was invited to sing. Right about that time, I also began to hear music and write new and original songs. They were born out of my love for the Lord and an intimacy that I experienced between God and me as I spent time in prayer and the word. These songs were different from the songs we sang in church. Again however, after I turned sixteen, my whole life as a born again believer changed after I was introduced to the charismatic community. The songs they sang were different too, but they reflected the same kind of intimacy and love for God as the music I was writing. And better still, that intimacy seemed to be a shared experience in the collective worship experience.

Minister Virginia talked about that difference during our interview. While attending college at University of Missouri at St. Louis, she founded a singing group called the University of Missouri Black Student Choir. She said that the group was originally founded in recognition of Black History month and traveled from one college campus to another, singing various forms of music. However, she said that the core group of students involved in the choir were young

Christians, therefore, the group eventually evolved into a full fledge gospel choir after their graduation.

According to Minister Martin, the gospel group was accustomed to singing in charismatic worship services, as well as traditional denominational worship services. She explained the difference as she said, "We would sing a song and people would get glad in the same way they would hoop and holler because someone is singing a song and they have good musical skill. And so the good musical skill and the ability to harmonize can move you, because music can move you. But with worship and praise, the experience is not the same as just being moved and hollering out. There is a difference in being moved and actually having a worship experience. The worship and praise music was a liberating type of experience that just singing some choir songs didn't give you. It puts you in a place of worship. And that worship experience has become an integral part of the worship service. So you see that aspect of praise and worship, we didn't have."

As I thought about the influence of contemporary praise and worship, and how it has impacted the church and touched the lives of individuals I have known, one particular example came to mind. It is the personal testimony of a respected brother and friend in Christ, whose testimony captures the essence of this subject, in its entirety. He is Pastor Brad Hirsch, pastor and the shepherd of a local Lutheran congregation in the St. Louis area. Pastor Hirsch is a graduate of Concordia Theological Seminary.

One day before going to work, I stopped by the church to talk with him and to ask for an interview. In his usual kind and gentle way, he invited me into his office and asked me to take a seat. I sat down in the chair opposite his desk and I couldn't help but notice the photographs of family members strategically placed round about the desktop. Across the room was a collection of Bibles, reference materials and books on spiritual guidance, and other religious topics. And even more conspicuously placed was a photo-collage of the families and kids of the congregation, new members and recent outreach activities. It was mounted on the wall, in line of sight directly adjacent to his desk. After a bit of small talk, I told him about the premise of my book and asked for an interview. He agreed and we began.

Pastor Hirsch began by saying, "I was introduced to praise and worship songs at a Lutheran camp in 1976. They were simple choruses and most were Bible verses. I even started to write a few, but I'm not very talented in the writing department. We sang them all summer long", he said with a smile as he reminisced. He continued, "My little brother, Ben left the LCMS and joined a Pentecostal church.

Although we disagreed theologically, our common ground besides Jesus was music. He sent me a tape by Vineyard fellowship. I wore it out I played it so much. I began to dive headlong into praise and worship style and even played guitar for a small charismatic group of Lutherans in Seattle in the 80's.

Brad says he collected Integrity Hosannas tapes and later CD's and began working with a pastor friend in Crescent City, California to form a praise band. As we continued our conversation, Pastor Hirsch said, "Our little church of about one hundred started a 'contemporary' format on a Sunday night. Not many people came. In fact, it was a failure, numbers wise. But we enjoyed the songs and worship among ourselves, and the few who came." As he recalled, he said that in those days, this style was just unheard of in Lutheran circles. He went on to say, "Anyway, after a year of a few people (a good night was 20), the pastor of the church asked the elders to add this service to the Sunday morning schedule. They said, 'OK. There's nothing to lose.' The typical Lutheran approach to a new idea was to try it for a time and see if it works. So we did a traditional service at 8 a.m. and a contemporary service at 10:30."

At this point, I interrupted the flow of conversation to ask if there was enough of a change in the attendance to consider it a success, or was it still considered to be a "failure" in his opinion. The pastor leaned forward in his chair and the pitch and tone of his voice seemed to raise an octave as he responded, "The attendance at that service (the contemporary service) doubled, tripled and soared! Many people came to Christ; many "worn out" Lutherans renewed their zeal. We were in the middle of a revival that reached into every corner of the church… youth, missions, music, volunteers, families, careers, etc. And to this day," Brad concluded, "it remains the most popular service and still reaches many people for Jesus." When I asked what made him leave such a wonderful ministry. He simply replied, "My wife, daughter, and I left Crescent City, California in 2000 to attend Seminary here in St. Louis because I felt God calling me to pastoral ministry."

The scenario that Pastor Hirsch described is typical of the influence and impact the charismatic music ministry has had upon the traditional church. Indeed, this is exactly what I have experienced among the churches that transitioned to a new contemporary format. We must ask the question why? What's the reason for the success of this phenomenal worship movement? Well, allow me to submit the following ideas as food for thought in our discussion.

The Power of the Word in Music

As the Reformation got under way, it was a song that helped bring everyone together. The hymn "A Mighty Fortress is our King" written by Martin Luther became the battle cry of the reformers in the 16th century. Luther believed that good theology set to common, basic musical tunes was the best way to get people to remember the principles of the word of God as they faced the struggles of life. His understanding of the power of music and His passion for truth helped to change the face of Christianity as he stood up against the corruption of the Catholic Church.

It was that same insight and passion that moved him to embrace the idea of employing a then contemporary style and method to express the timeless truth of scripture in a fresh, new and engaging way. It was from the same spirit of insight and passion that modern day contemporary worship and praise was born. I believe the impact of the new charismatic worship style of our day, is just as important for the Word of Faith message and movement, as the contemporary approach that Martin Luther used to spread the message of grace through faith for his day. For in very much the same way, contemporary praise and worship has helped to bring about a reformation of worship for today's Church.

Songs We Sing on Media Screens

Back in 1980, when I attended my very first Sunday mourning Charismatic worship service, one of the things I was most fascinated by was the use of an overhead projector during the worship service.

At my former church, I had been accustomed to following along in a hymnal book, gazing upon a Xerox copy, or simply listening until I caught on to enough of the words and melody to sing along with the rest of the congregation. But this! This was something altogether new and different! As I made my way between the rows to be seated, I looked to the front of the church, and what I saw was the coolest thing I had ever seen in church. Just above the pulpit, on either side of the wall, was a projected image of the words for the song to be sung. And with each transition to another song, there appeared a new display of lyrics, in larger than life view for all to see.

At that time, that was big stuff for a sixteen-year-old kid, from an inner city, old-school Pentecostal church. However, after more than twenty-five years later, I still surprised to see how many churches have incorporated visual aid technology into their worship service. Media screens and overhead projection displays have become a trademark signature of the Charismatic Church. In fact, churches around the world have adopted this technology. This is a sure indicator of the incredible influence of the charismatic community upon the church at large.

Consider the fact that the generation that emerged from the Sixties had attended college, and now had entered the workforce. Then it is quite understandable how this visual aid tool made the transition from the classroom and boardroom, to the people of God in the "upper room". I believe that this was not simply a coincidence. The Bible says, "In the fullness of time, Christ came…" In the very same manner, God chose that time and season in history to introduce this technology into the Church.

Why? For what reason would God allow this technology to be incorporated into the church? I believe the purpose was to promote oneness and unity in worship, because it would help to bring about an answer to a prayer by our Lord and Savior, Jesus Christ. According to John 17:20-22, Jesus prayed that we would be made one with God, Himself and with one another. Therefore, God has introduced this instrument to he body of Christ to encourage and assist its members in the process of unity and oneness.

The biblical principle is the "unity of the Spirit" that King David talked about in Psalms 133. It is this anointing that we see released in the company of those who were gathered together "with one accord in one place." (Acts 2: 9-11) It was truly a mixed group of people, brought together under the anointed umbrella of the Spirit of unity. It is in the same Spirit of anointed unity that people assemble with one accord to give God praise expressed in charismatic worship services. Just like the cloven tongues of fire that appeared above the heads of men and women gathered together in the upper room represented a bright and visual light of unification, the illuminated images of scriptural lyrics projected on media screens are used to encourage an atmosphere of unity. When believers within the charismatic community began to practice and experience this kind of worship, the effects were no different than those found in Acts chapter two. Verse 46 says, "So continuing daily with one accord … the Lord added to the Church daily those who were being saved." This is the result and explanation for the exponential growth of the Charismatic Church.

By Divine Design

One of the most important and influential aspects of Contemporary Praise and Worship, is that built into this style of worship, is an expectation and understanding that God desires to meet and commune with His people. Psalm 63: 2-4 says, *"So, I have looked for You in the sanctuary, to see Your power and Your glory. Because Your loving-kindness is better than life, my lips shall praise You. Thus I will bless You while I live; I will lift up my hands in Your name."*

From the earliest days of the Charismatic movement, an emphasis has been placed upon the importance of understanding the truth of scripture regarding praise. In passages such as Psalm 47:6, 7 we are admonished to *"Sing praises with understanding."* Therefore, teaching based on passages that declare who God is, how He is enthroned and exalted, and how He lives, dwells, and inhabits the praises of his people (Psalm 22:3), helped to establish an understanding of God's position and place in praise. Other key scriptures like Psalm 29:2 *"Worship the Lord in the beauty of holiness"* helped to lay a foundation about God's desire for holiness and intimacy in worship.

Word of Faith teachers instructed us to *"Put on the garment of praise for the spirit of heaviness"*, as stated by the prophet Isaiah. (Isaiah 61:3) Still other passages such Psalm 33:1, which exhorts us to rejoice because *"praise is comely for the upright"*, helped to provide clarity about the role of praise and worship in the life of the believer. To help us relate, one teacher aptly said, "Praise looks good on you!" As a result, the people of God learned to anticipate and wait on the manifested glory of His presence (Psalm 33:20). Therefore, through divine purpose and design, this genre of music seeks to create and facilitate an atmosphere of holy reverence and expectation for the presence of God.

Consider the example of the children of Israel in the days of Moses. When the congregation of Israel was called upon to prepare to meet with God, they literally expected to meet with and experience, the manifested presence of the Holy One of Israel! There was a real anticipation that God was about to visit the congregation of His chosen people. This distinctive quality and influential attribute was reintroduced to the body of Christ through contemporary worship and praise. This was very different from the atmosphere created by many of the more traditional worship services, which seemed to leave very little room, and even less expectation for a visit from the glorious presence of God. Instead, they seemed to be content with a "business as usual", type of climate for worship service.

During my interview with Pastor Hirsch, he commented on this very issue. He explained, "There was never an attempt to change the liturgy or bring in new songs because we were taught other expressions were un-biblical. In those days, and some still today believe that to be truly Lutheran you must worship the only correct way, and that is TLH (Today's Lutheran Hymnal). Any other way, and your Lutheran heritage was questioned and possibly your faith in Christ." It's no wonder that so many would come to church and leave the same way, in the same un-regenerated and un-rejuvenated condition in which they came.

The word of God says that, "God inhabits the praises of His people", therefore there is no way that one can experience the glory of the presence of God and remain unchanged. This is the message, method and ministry of contemporary praise and worship. It conveys the message of God's holiness, glory and majesty, and the sense of awe and wonder that is felt, as the creation responds to the Creator. The message of the cross is also prominent within the lyrical content of contemporary worship, with an emphasis on the love of God for His people, and particularly the individual worshiper.

Again, this is where modern praise and worship is very effective because it creates an atmosphere that uniquely facilitates and intentionally incorporates the dual nature of worship for the believer. While it effectively promotes and emphasizes the call to corporate worship, it also assists and encourages the believer to engage in the worship service and experience it in a very personal and intimate way. Therein, lays the beauty, simplicity and popularity of this style of worship. This characteristic can largely be attributed to the method used to create this form of worship style and musical expression.

Pastor Brad recalled that "Things began to change in the 70's and now we have what is called, worship wars." You see we are not so divided about Christ and his redemptive work. However when it gets beyond the basics, then we tend to disagree regarding secondary issues not pertinent to our salvation. Issues such as baptism, music and style of worship are given such importance that they become catalyst for division. It's my prayer that we can develop an appreciation and positive affirmation for the different gifts and callings administered by God to each denomination within the body of Christ, including the gifts introduced through the charismatic community.

Contemporary Style and Design

From the introduction of acrylic podiums and semi circular seating to overhead projected song lyrics and media screens. There is a distinctive style associated with the Charismatic Church and its influence upon the church at large. Just as it was in the days of Davidic temple preparation, and during the artistic influence of the Renaissance, today's gifted designers and architects have been given an opportunity to create some of the most beautifully designed and distinctive worship centers of our day.

By combining contemporary styling with ergonomic form and function, together the latest technology, enormous size and structural beauty, today's artisans created and build modern day works of art. Some may ask what these things have to do with worship. The answer is simple. Since we are to worship and praise God for all that he is, then we must acknowledge that He is the God of Beauty, a God of design and flawless function. Therefore, He is to be praised for every aspect of beauty and magnificence we find.

Architectural Design and Influence

One day, while listening to noted theologian R.C. Sproul's radio broadcast, I listened as he talked about Christianity and its influence upon the Arts[10]. On that particular evening, one of the topics he addressed was Christian influence upon architecture (church architecture in particular). During his discussion, he established that the goal of ancient and medieval builders was to inspire and promote the message of the holiness and splendor of God. He mentioned the fact that he believed that the modern church has lost its sense of the "holy". He then stated that he felt today's architects and builders no longer approach the task of building a church with the intent to inspire and promote the message of God's holiness and splendor. Finally he asked the question, "If this is not the message that church architects wish to convey, then what is the message that is communicated by the churches and worship centers of today?

Ironically, I had been thinking about this very subject in preparation for this book. Dr. Sproul's analysis and question really helped to organize and solidify my thoughts and views for a more apologetic response. I believe for the most part, that it is not the intent of modern day church architects and designers of contemporary worship centers to simply forsake the traditions and influences, which inspired builders from the Roman and Gothic periods. Nor have they intentionally chosen to distance their designs from the feeling of "churchliness" and "holiness" in an effort to simply become more ergonomic and utilitarian in the designs.

As a matter of fact, I believe the message communicated by modern day artisans and builders is no different than their medieval counter parts. Most certainly, it is to reflect and display the beauty, splendor and wonders of our creator. However, the method and style in which it is achieved is the greatest point of difference and departure. Instead of representing the holiness of God from an Old Testament style of opulence and grandeur, contemporary designer/builders communicate this message with a New Testament style that embraces the beauty and wonder of the divine-human relationship. Rather than emphasizing the great divide between the Creator and His creation, they underscore the message of Christ's love and miracle of the redemptive work, as it was embodied and expressed through the commonality of mankind.

Instead of seeking to emphasize the holiness of God through intricate stained glass windows and lofty cathedral ceilings, modern day designers seek to emphasize the holy and divine miracle of God's presence among men. Rather than perpetuating the Old Testament message of an unapproachable God and His veiled sacred space, they seek to communicate the New Testament message of love and acceptance; with design styles intended to encourage and underscore the invitation of fellowship and intimacy through the glorious gospel of Christ.

Therefore, such inspiration might appear at first glance to be less God-centered, or less glorious and even profane, but in reality it could not be further from the truth. Today's churches and worship centers are designed to communicate, facilitate and accentuate the divine worship experience in such a way that is God-focused, Christ centered and Holy Spirit filled. In a very real and literal sense, these designs are intended to promote the communion between a Holy God and the people whom He has called to be His holy people. We have been called to worship Him! These new sanctuaries and worship settings emphasize the call to worship, and facilitate an atmosphere of expectation for the sacred presence and power of the Holy One.

Semi-Circle Seating

As we consider the design of contemporary sanctuaries and worship center auditoriums, allow me to draw your attention to the place to which God called His people together to receive the Commandments of God. The place was Mount Sinai and the twelve tribes of Israel were instructed to encamp around the mountain. That instruction placed the mountain logistically in the "center" of the people. Therefore, the delivery of the Commandments and instructions were issued from a central focal point within the camp. This configuration illustrates the central focus and place of prominence the Word of God should have in our worship camp. I believe this is the design message conveyed by the semi-circle seating arrangements found in many charismatic worship centers. The Word should take center stage within our life.

Ok. Some may say, "Well that's an Old Testament illustration! We are no longer under the law, but under grace. Are there any New Testament examples?" In response to your query, the answer is a resounding "yes"! We find our ultimate example in the person of Jesus, recorded in Matthew 5:1. It says, ***"And seeing the multitude, He went up on a mountain, and when He was seated, His disciples came to Him. Then He taught them saying…"*** In this example, like Moses, Jesus takes a position atop the mountain to teach the Word of God and to instruct the people. Those who followed Him (His disciples) came to Him "around the mountain" to hear the word of the Lord.

This example is again illustrated in Matthew 15:29, 30 where Jesus has compassion on the multitude. He not only healed them, he also sat them down (around the mountain) and fed them. So, we see the picture of Jesus the Bread of life, ministering the children's bread of healing, to those who were camped around the mountain. Then He feeds them by multiplying seven loaves of natural bread and some fish, to minister to their natural need of for food.

Therefore, we have an established biblical precedent for the model we find in the modern contemporary worship centers of our day. They are designed to emulate this model of "gathering round about" to receive the word of God, from the messenger of God. And to facilitate the presence of God to bring healing for the spirit, soul and body of believers who follow Him to the mountain.

Chapter Five
SEMINARY THEOLOGY FOR LAYMEN

Without a doubt, I believe that the greatest contribution and most significant gift given to the Church via the charismatic experience, was an outpour of the teaching gift upon the body of Christ. Since the mid to late 1970's, there has been a new anointing and emphasis placed upon the gift of teaching. Through this unprecedented outpour, God has brought a greater understanding of His word, to the Christian masses. Particularly to those who were less likely to be exposed to the quality and level of teaching, that at one time, was only available through seminary education.

The first time I attended a charismatic worship service, I saw something that was very different from the traditional worship service I was accustomed to. I noticed that everyone had a pen and notepad along with a Bible. As the speaker taught from the scriptures, I could see that the person to my right and on my left would jot down notes related to the sermon. And after a few weeks of fellowship, something else became clearly evident to me. The people didn't seem to study just to gain intellectual information, nor did their attendance appear to stem from legalistic obligation. Instead, it seemed to flow from a passionate desire to gain a more intimate acquaintance and better understanding of the God they loved and the Christ they followed.

Each time we gathered, there seemed to be an attitude of expectancy and gladness that filled the room. They were genuinely excited about God and what He had done for them, and even more about what He had promised to do for them! Best of all, God was truly faithful. For just as the people's hunger increased, so did God's provision to feed them through an explosion of the gift of teaching. Almost over night, it seemed that God began to raise up men and women within the body of Christ who were not only skilled in preaching the word, but were also able to teach it, explain and convey it in a practical and understandable manner. These men and women seemed to have an anointing that enabled them to bring the word of God alive in such a way that was absolutely exciting to hear. It was truly a word of faith that was personally applicable and completely relevant for our time. As teaching ministries began to flourish and our exposure to the word increased, our knowledge and understanding began to grow also.

As a matter of fact, a new phrase was coined in an effort to describe the churches born out of such ministries. They became known as "Word" churches. Suddenly, principles and concepts once confined within the walls of seminaries and other theological institutions of higher learning were now being taught on a regular basis, to common everyday Christians. It was theology for the masses, with an understanding of terms like justification, sanctification and propitiation took on an entirely new point of relevance and importance.

Teaching with a Different Slant

As my wife and I sat in the cozy kitchen of Sister Virginia's warm suburban home, I asked what initially attracted her to the Charismatic or Word of Faith community. She paused for a moment before responding. Then, in an effort to find just the right words she said, "Um! I hadn't thought about it before." After a moment of silence, she continued by saying, "The teaching and the freedom. But not just the teaching, it was a different slant on the teaching."

Of course, we had to ask what she meant by the phrase, "a different slant?"

As we continued the conversation, she carefully elaborated on her answer, with the following response. "Different in that, you can take some teaching and just go down the line and I don't care what denomination you're in, the basic Evangelical teaching of the gospel was the same. But then there were areas that were not addressed. The faith, the not being in poverty, and as black people in America, being entrenched in poverty, it was a message for us; young people who were striving to come out of poverty."

Again she paused for a moment of reflective clarity, so I took the opportunity to interject a question. "So were they addressed in the Charismatic Word-Faith teaching?" I asked. Then she responded, "Well, …addressed because, even though I had received the baptism of the Holy Spirit, I did not have any real teaching (about the Holy Spirit) other than the Holy Ghost was power. But there was more to that thing. And they (the Word of Faith teachers) delved into questions like: What were the functions? What was the purpose? How did that relate to your life and how could that be used in your life?

So that was an area and an entirely different slant on the Holy Spirit. That's why I say *slant* on the Holy Spirit! Because, yes...I did know that the Holy Spirit was for today and that you could receive the baptism, and I'd learned that. And I received it. But there was another aspect, that other aspect ... that different slant, where they taught some things that went deeper. And it caused me to grow deeper in God more quickly than I believe I would have."

Sister Virginia's testimony is a perfect example of the difference that helped define the Word of Faith experience for so many more individuals who were hungry for the kind of in-depth teaching that simply was not available from most traditional denominational churches of that day. Indeed, this may be the single most important ingredient in the Charismatic recipe for supernatural success. It was the propensity to preach and teach the word of God in a practical and applicable manner that got folks turned on to the bible. As people got turned on to the Word, they in turn became stronger, better equipped and better able to live the Christian life. Of course, that was part of God's plan from day one; that the body of Christ would be strengthened and edified through the preaching and teaching of the gospel.

The Focus Factor

Probably the biggest difference between the preaching and teaching of the Word of Faith community and traditional Evangelical Christian camps is an issue of emphasis and focus. Although it may be a bit difficult to explain, it can most certainly be seen and understood by attending a traditional service on any given Sunday morning, followed by attendance of a nondenominational service the next Sunday. After uttering the very first prayer and song that begins the worship service, one will immediately notice the difference in the emphasis placed upon various elements of the Christian faith. Keep in mind that these elements are accepted as orthodox teachings in all Christian communities. However, the difference is simply one of focus and emphasis placed upon certain fundamentals of the faith.

For instance, the focus of most Evangelical teaching is on Christ's suffering, His cross at Calvary, and our position and response as sinners to the message of the gospel. The emphasis of the songs, prayers and teaching is usually focused upon the depraved and sinful nature of the human condition apart from Christ. And usually there is not much of a delineation made between the believer and the unbeliever, other than the fact that we are sinners saved by grace. The message from the point of emphasis says, "Yes. We are saved by grace through faith in Christ alone, but we are still sinners none the less."

However, when attending a Charismatic service, one will notice that the songs, prayers and message are usually focused on the same elements of Christianity, but there is an intentional effort to broaden the focus. Therefore, the spotlight of worship is expanded to include an emphasis on the greatness, majesty and splendor of God the Creator. The focal point is enlarged to include the celebration of our love for God in addition to our appreciation for His love toward us.

Because we are His children, the focus of worship reflects our celebration of His loving-kindness, goodness and tender mercy. This celebration is expressed throughout the worship experience in song, prayer, preaching and teaching. However, this does not in any way diminish the preeminence and Lordship of Jesus Christ. The focus is most certainly on Christ and His suffering, His death, burial and resurrection. But the emphasis does not end there, as it is also placed upon His life and ministry after the cross.

Consequently, the focus also shifts for those who receive salvation; it's not just about coming to the cross, but life after the cross as well. For the sinful man, this means that the need and requirements for salvation are clearly taught and emphasized. Again however, the focus of teaching is not placed solely upon salvation, but also upon how to live life "after the cross", once you have received salvation. The teaching is then geared toward an understanding of the transition from sinner to saint, the translation from the kingdom of darkness to the kingdom of light, and the difference in the divine-human relationship; having been a slave to sin, but now, having been made a son of righteousness.

These are all key elements of fundamental orthodox Christianity, but it is the difference of focus and emphasis that separates Charismatic teaching from the traditional Evangelical message. We can see from the Bible that this approach is quite consistent with the teaching of scripture, possibly even more consistent. When we look at the writings of the Apostle Paul, his emphasis was always upon what Christ has done for us, what he has made us to be and what are to become, rather than what we once were.

In the Spirit of Wisdom and Revelation

In the first chapter of the book of Ephesians, we are introduced to the Apostle Paul's prayer for the church at Ephesus. Beginning at verse fifteen we read, *"Therefore I also, after I heard of your faith in the Lord Jesus and your love for all the saints, do not cease to give thanks for you, making mention of you in my prayers: that the God of our Lord Jesus Christ, the Father of glory, may give to you the spirit of wisdom and revelation in the knowledge of Him, the eyes of your understanding being enlightened; that you may know what is the hope of His calling, what are the riches of the glory of His inheritance in the saints, and what is the exceeding greatness of His power toward us who believe..."* (Ephesians 1:15-19)

Paul knew that his letters were read and circulated throughout the other churches in the region. Therefore, he most certainly intended the application to be universal among believers. It is also clear that there have been times throughout history when the answer to his prayer was hindered and even seemed impossible. One example of just such a time in history would be the period referred to as the Dark Ages.

After the loss of the Great Library at Alexandria, many books of antiquity were destroyed by fire. This catastrophic event, coupled with the fall of the Roman Empire, cast Europe into a period of intellectual, spiritual, social and political darkness and despair. This included the spiritual dimension because many manuscript copies of scriptural text were lost. As a result, the Roman Church seized all remaining text and declared them to be too scarce, too sacred and too holy for the common man to read. This unfortunate turn of events ended the possession and circulation of scripture throughout the western civilized world. Consequently, this removed God's word from the hands of common people and placed it under the strict control of Church leaders and theologians.

Considering the circulation of ancient manuscript copies and early church epistles throughout the first few centuries of church history, the period of the Dark Ages certainly represent a striking antithesis to the Pauline prayer for revelation and enlightenment. But God is faithful to answer the faintest reverberated echo of His word. Therefore, the period of the Reformation represents the fruitful answer to Paul's prayer for Christians. With a new vision for the fulfillment of Paul's prayer, men fought to return the possession of sacred scripture to the hands of common folk. Such individuals must certainly be regarded as heroes of the faith and examples of God's faithfulness.

Now then, as we fast-forward to today, the Bible says, *"The effective, fervent prayers of a righteous man avails much* (James 5:16)." Therefore it is the same Spirit of wisdom and revelation in the knowledge of our Lord Jesus, spoken of in Paul's prayer, that brought illumination and revelation to the body of Christ in our day. As men and women of faith poured out their heart and soul before God in prayer and fasting, God responded in faithfulness, mercy and compassion, and He answered the cry of His people. And what was the cry of His people? All across the globe, from every culture and denomination, the cry from many was that they simply wanted more. More of God, more of His wisdom and knowledge, more of His spirit, more of His presence and power, and to experience more of His love!

So, God responded by rising up men and women, full of faith and power. And in whom was the spirit of wisdom and revelation from His word. Then He released them into the body of Christ, through nondenominational churches and Word of Faith ministries, to bring illumination and recovery of sight to the blind. They did so by taking the teaching and understanding of God's word from the traditional confines of theological seminaries and making it accessible and understandable for the common layperson. Although some will disagree, I find surprising correlations between the printing and distribution of the Bible for the masses of Europe in the 1600's, and the latter day outpouring of the Spirit of wisdom and revelation knowledge of our time. Both movements were inspired by God to provide access to information that was once reserved for clergy and students of theology to the masses.

Sheik to Speak Greek

One of the most memorable aspects of the new hunger to understand the Bible was the desire to become familiar with the original languages of the scriptures. To say the least, this kind of in depth study was unheard of in most traditional, old-school denominational churches of the day. However, when Word of Faith preachers and teachers began to incorporate this information into their Bible studies and Sunday morning sermons, the affect was phenomenal. Suddenly, everyone wanted to know the original Greek word or term for key words, as they studied passages from New Testament scriptures.

At first, they began to explain the use of certain words like *agape* (God's unconditional love) and *Zoë* (the life of God or God's kind of life), teaching us the origin, the original definitions, meanings and intent of such words, and how they related to the believer as a child of God. Suddenly, it was sheik to speak Greek! The overall impact of this kind of information was immeasurable and invaluable in terms of the wealth of knowledge, wisdom and power available to the believer. Our ability to comprehend and understand the word of God increased, due to this new style of teaching. It was revolutionary because it provided seminary theology for ordinary laymen.

Next, there was the increased popularity of resource material and new study Bibles that specifically suited this style of teaching. One case in point was the introduction of the Amplified Bible, with its exhaustive exposition of every key word and phrase, designed to deliver insightful information and definitions for every scriptural reference. Everywhere you looked, one could find someone in the group who had an "Amplified". It single handedly helped to change the way many charismatic believers read, studied and taught the Bible. Not to mention the increased popularity of resources like the Vine's Greek Dictionary and the Strong's Concordance and their profound influence upon Charismatic Christians. Such tools for study helped to both fuel and satisfy the insatiable desire to know and understand more of the word of God.

The affects of this charismatic influence upon other members of the body of Christ is quite apparent. For instance, when my wife and I recently attended a small Baptist church in our community, it was an interesting experience. The minister made several references to Greek and Hebrew words and their meanings. As we listened to the message, I could not help but remember the days when that kind of information would not have been part of a Baptist sermon. I believe the increased popularity and pervasive incorporation of Greek and Hebrew terminology into denominational preaching and teaching is a direct result of the influence of charismatic-style teaching upon the body of Christ. In my opinion this has been a very good thing.

Rebirth of the Berean Spirit

In Acts 17:10-12 we are introduced to a group of Jewish converts in the city of Berea. These first-century believers were unique in their response to the message that Paul and Silas preached. As the record of the account begins in verse ten, we are told that when the men of God arrived in the city, they went to the synagogue to meet the Jews of Berea. Verse eleven immediately describes these Jewish believers as *"more fair-minded,"* or noble, than the Jews of Thessalonica. This is the first point of difference and distinction used to describe the Berean converts.

The second point of distinction tells us why they were different. The remainder of verse eleven says that they were different, *"in that they received the word with all readiness, and searched the Scriptures daily to find out whether these things were so."* I believe it is extremely interesting to note that this description is not given for anyone else. First of all, it says they received the word with all readiness. This shows us the attitude of the Berean heart as the preaching of the Word fell upon good fertile ground.

Next we see the priority given to the authority of Scripture, because they searched daily to find out whether the things which Paul and Silas preached to them were true. This reveals a truly sincere desire, on their part, to know and understand the truth of Gods word for their selves. I find it quite interesting, given the credibility of the Apostle Paul testimony; the Jews of Berea did not simply take his word for it. But rather, they took the time and energy to investigate the claims Paul made, and compared them to the truth of Scripture. The end result of their investigative effort is recorded for us in verse twelve where it says, ***"Therefore many of them believed, and also not a few Greeks, prominent women as well as men."*** Wow! So we see that it wasn't just the Jews who were convinced, but also common citizens and influential members of the Greek community were converted as well. This certainly speaks to the power of the gospel unto salvation.

I believe that the relative difference and distinctions drawn in this passage are fascinating when compared to the modern day charismatic experience of our time. It is a fitting description of the difference and distinction that characterized the charismatic community from it beginning. One of the greatest blessings to come out of the Charismatic Movement was an explosion of the desire to know the word of God and to understand it in a greater measure. During the early 1970's and '80's, there was an insatiable hunger for the Word of God. It swept across the nondenominational community and into the homes and churches of common folk everywhere. Suddenly, in small home based study groups, young people were actually excited about reading the Bible. They weren't just reading the Bible, they were studying the Bible!

I mentioned earlier in a previous chapter about how my first encounter with a charismatic study group left me eager to get into my own biblical study of the topics and principles discussed on that evening. In hindsight, I suppose a real motivation for my eager interest was due in part to the gentleman who led the bible study on that night. He insisted that we should read and study the Bible to find out for ourselves, just what the Word said, and that we shouldn't simply take his or anyone else's word for it.

What I experienced was not the response of just that local study group, but rather, it was the typical response within such charismatic groups. That kind of encouragement was characteristic of preachers and teachers associated with the Word of Faith movement. It did not matter weather the group was a small study group or a mega church congregation. It was common to see people with their bibles open, with pen and pad in hand, taking notes as the preacher or teacher ministered the Word of God.

✝

Chapter Six

MIRACLES FOR THE MUNDANE

Around the time I was introduced to the charismatic community, just before I left the denominational church I attended, I experienced another encounter that had a profound impact upon my Christian life. About mid summer of 1979 or '80, our little inner city Pentecostal church ran a weeklong revival meeting. Of course this was not the first revival meeting the church had, but it was the first of its kind I had ever encountered.

During this particular meeting, something wonderful and unexpected happened. The church invited a young minister to speak whom we had not met before. He was a tall thin Word-Faith preacher with a dark complexion and big hands. I remember his hands because every time he prayed for someone, it reminded me of an NBA player holding the basketball in the grasp of his long-fingered hand. However, I quickly got beyond that distraction, as he preached the message of faith to our small congregation.

After about the third night of the revival, he asked if anyone wanted prayer for healing. He instructed those who stood to their feet to come down front to receive prayer. To my surprise, he asked if I would accompany him, as he laid hands on those who wanted prayer. To say the least, I was a bit nervous, but I was more than willing to assist because it was the first time I was asked to assist in such a grownup way. Little did I know, that my faith in what God could do was about to increase, by a hundredfold.

From the back of the sanctuary came an elderly woman who attended the church quite frequently. Most of the time, she walked to church because she lived about three or four blocks from the church. Almost everyone, including me and my family, thought that it was just a little too far to walk, because she walked with a limp. But she hardly ever accepted a ride to or from her destination. As the lady made her way down the isle to the front of the church, the young minister and I patiently waited for her to join us.

When she finally arrived, the minister smiled and greeted her, as he welcomed her to the place of prayer. He then quietly asked what she wanted God to do for her. By now, for some reason she had begun to cry, and through the tears she replied, "I just want the Lord to touch my body." After she said this, the young minister reached out and gently took both her hands and told her that the Lord wanted to do exactly that, and even more. He then turned his attention to the congregation. They had already begun to pray as he asked the question, "How many of you believe that tonight God wants to give this lady a miracle?" The congregation responded with a hardy Amen and began to clap their hands in agreement.

Next, the minister turned to me and asked if I would go get two chairs for her to set in. Of course I agreed and quickly nabbed a couple of chairs from the pastor's office, and returned at once. On the way back, I wondered why he requested two chairs since she was the only person that came up for prayer. But I really didn't think much beyond the request. When I returned, the minister asked her to set down in one chair, and then he placed both of her feet in the seat of the other. The woman had always worn an orthopedic shoe on one foot. You know the kind that had a thicker sole than the other one. Everyone could see that one leg was about two to three inches shorter than the other. After that, things really began to get interesting!

Without any further ado, he laid his hands upon her head and began to pray. I also placed my hand upon her shoulder and lifted the other toward heaven. But in all honesty, I was completely unprepared and surprised by what happened next. As we prayed with her, the leg that was shorter than the other began to grow longer, in plain sight and view for all to see! Not all at once, but in three visually distinct increments; the first of which happened suddenly without warning. The next incremental growth was about a good inch, which happened much slower but just as surprisingly. Finally, the last growth spurt produced about another half-inch or so in length. What I noticed, almost as if it were in slow motion, was the way in which the final increment of growth gradually extended her foot far enough to be perfectly equal with the other. It was nothing less than miraculous! Amazingly, it all happened over the course of about three to four minutes! I was so blown away, I didn't know what to think or say, except to keep on praying and thanking the Lord at a volume that was just above a whisper. By the time we were through praying for her, I was so ecstatic that my prayer turned to praise and the sound of my voice grew louder! I had never seen anything like it in all my life.

When that little old mother of the church finally realized exactly what had happened, her expression of excitement said it all. She began to cry even more as she screamed at the top of lungs and yelled, "THANK YOU JESUS...THANK YOU JESUS...THANK YOU JESUS!" over and over again. As she swung her feet off of the opposite chair and down onto the red carpeted floor, she sat there for the next few minutes, looking down at her feet while repeatedly rubbing her legs then clapping her hands in succession. After which she simply got up and began to run around the outer isles of the sanctuary at least two or three times. By the time she finished and returned back to the front of the church, the entire congregation was in tears and in praise!

And as for me, I would never be the same. Not only did the Lord touch that little old mother of the church on that warm summer evening, He also touched me! I truly learned that evening that with God, all things are possible. Again, I say it was nothing less than miraculous! After that revival meeting, I never had the opportunity to see that young minister again, but needless to say, his ministry and message on that night left an indelible impression upon my life.

Model for Miraculous Ministry

Many of our intellectual Evangelical Christian brethren like to identify with the ministry of the Apostle Paul, because of his unequalled apologetic prowess. Although Paul's apologetic ability is most certainly admirable, and should inspire others to want to emulate this aspect of his ministry, however Paul's apologetic ability should not be the only aspect of his ministry to be emulated. Intellectual Christian elites will probably disagree, but I believe men like Smith Wigglesworth and Kenneth Hagin also personify an important aspect of Paul's ministry. In fact, Paul's declaration in his address to the Corinthian church in 1 Corinthians 2:1-4, is the embodiment of what Wigglesworth's ministry was all about. In this passage, Paul begins by saying *"I did not come to you with excellency of speech, but in the demonstration of power."* Therefore, if we are going to identify with Paul and his ministry, we must be willing to embrace the full measure of what he represented. For it is nothing less than an example of the full measure of Christ's model for ministry.

To illustrate this point, let's look at the fourteenth chapter of Acts, where Paul and Barnabas preached the gospel to both Jews and Greeks. Remember now that the Jews are the religious and spiritual leaders and the Greeks are the pagan intellectuals of the day. In verse one [1] we read that Paul and Barnabas *"spoke so that a great multitude of both Jews and Greeks believed."* The passage continues, *"But unbelieving Jews stirred up the gentiles by poisoning their minds against the brethren. Therefore they stayed there a long time."*

Why did they stay and what were they doing? The passage tells us that Paul and Barnabas stayed there to preach and teach the word of God, *"speaking boldly in the Lord, who was bearing witness to His word."* At this point, I believe it is important to note just how the Lord bore witness to His word. The remainder of the verse explains that God did so, *"by granting signs and wonders to be done by their hands."*

So we see Paul and Barnabas engaging in several ministerial gifts. First we read that they preached a stirring Pentecostal message in the presentation of the gospel. Next it says that they presented a solid intellectual apologetic argument to Jews and Greeks who opposed them. And finally, God gave them the kind of charismatic grace that confirmed the preaching and teaching of the word, with signs and wonders.

My question is where did Paul and Barnabas learn this method of ministry? Where did Paul get it? I believe we can find the answer to this question elsewhere in Scripture. Consider the fact that he urges the Corinthians to follow him and imitate him as he follows Christ. (1 Corinthians 4:16) Therefore his example was Jesus, who demonstrated the same model for ministry. Jesus preached stirring messages, and confirmed the word He taught and preached with signs and wonders, then engaged the religious leaders with an intelligent apologetic response to their misguided intellectual arguments. As Jesus commissioned his disciples and sent them out into ministry, this was the method and model they were instructed to use when He said, "Heal the sick, raise the dead and cast out devils," just as Jesus Himself had done.

Confidence thru Biblical History

Many critics argue that God no longer performs miracles by the hands of men, while others say that the age of miracles ended with the book of Acts and is no longer the way in which God works. To respond to these arguments, we must again return to the authority of scripture for our response. Throughout the Old and New Testament, the Bible is filled with accounts of miracles, signs and wonders, literally from Genesis to Revelation. Since we have established the fact that as believers, we must accept the authenticity and authority of scripture as the final standard of truth, we must in turn accept the accounts of those miracles, signs and wonders as actual historic accounts.

One source of credible evidence is the historic information that supports the charismatic position for miracles throughout biblical history. First of all, let's consider the biblical historic evidence available to us from the pages of scripture. One example would be the miracles wrought by the hand of Moses. From the transformation of the staff into a serpent and back to a staff again, to the parting of the Red Sea, the biblical record states that God performed miraculous wonders through His servant Moses.

There is also the record of the prophets found in the Old Testament books of Joshua through Esther. These books are known as historic books that were taken from the Torah and span about seven hundred years of Old Testament history of the Jewish people. These books alone are filled with accounts of the many miracles performed by the men of God. For example, consider the account of the Prophet Elisha recorded in the book of 2 Kings. The deeds of this man of God included the miracle of an increase in the widows oil, found in chapter four, verses one through seven of 2 Kings. There is also the miracle of the conception and resurrection of the son of the Shunammite woman, and the miracle of the multiplication of the loaves recorded in verses 42 through 44.

I believe that it was quite by divine intent that those miracles mirror the accounts of Jesus found throughout the pages of the New Testament gospels. The miracles of Jesus include the feeding of the five thousand with two fish and five loaves, resurrecting the young girl and His friend Lazarus, the transformation of water to wine, and the many other miracles of healing. If God is indeed the same yesterday, today and forever, then He is the same God of the miraculous now, as He was then. That is exactly what scripture proclaims Him to be.

Therefore, since God has performed miracles throughout the entire history of the biblical record, then it stands to reason that He is still able and willing to perform miracles in the lives of men and women today. This is just an example of the kind of response and line of defense we must use to engage the opposition from skeptics and critics alike. And with this kind of information and understanding, charismatic believers can be encouraged and strengthened.

From the earliest days of the Charismatic Movement, this has been the model for ministry that we have embraced. We can find confidence and take courage in the fact that the biblical historic record supports the charismatic position, which believes and teaches that God is still the God of the miraculous. We believe and teach exactly what Jesus taught when He said, *"nothing shall be impossible to him that believes"* and that God will do exceedingly, and abundantly above all we ask or think.

Confidence thru Church History

The book of Acts opens with a declaration by the author, which states that it is an accurate account of the birth and supernatural endowment, of the new religious and spiritual institution called the

Church. The history of the formative years of the Church is presented to us, through the inspired words of Luke, a physician and gentile disciple, who reported the events that surrounded the beginning of a new era in history. Luke's report covers the pages of twenty-eight chapters and spans a time period of about thirty years. It records the transformation of the eleven remaining disciples into the Twelve Apostle, by the power of the Holy Spirit on the Day of Pentecost, and ends with the Apostle Paul's trip to Rome, as he awaits trail just before 62 A.D.

Over the course of that thirty year period, we are again presented with accounts of miraculous events and deeds that helped to define the message of the gospel and characterized the ministry of the men and women who became the foundation of the new Christian movement. From the first recorded miracles of the resurrection and ascension of Christ in Acts 1:1-11, and Peter and John's encounter with the lame man at the temple gate, who received the miracle of healing at the command of the Apostle Peter to *"rise up and walk,"* to the unusual miracles God performed by the hands of Paul as the sick received healing from handkerchiefs and aprons that were sent from Paul's body, to his miraculous death defying encounter with the fireside serpent in Acts 28; the account of each miracle event is recorded and presented as historical fact.

Therefore, these facts must be included, as evidence for the type of power in ministry that accompanied the message and ministry of the first-century believers. Many critics of the charismatic community deny the continuation of the charismatic gifts of miracles beyond the first-century church, claiming that such ability has ceased and is no longer available to the Church. However, since Jesus never made a distinction between the early disciples and those who would come after them, their claim is speculative and unfounded at best because the evidence suggests that charismatic miracles continued well beyond the lives and ministry of the original founders of the Church.

Although the Bible is our primary source for authoritative documented information, it must not be the only source for credible documented information. There are plenty of extra-biblical sources that contain historic information about the history of Christianity, which may be presented in the argument for our defense.

Case in point; consider the report of St. Gregory the Great, who was pope from about 590 to 604 A.D. St. Gregory wrote a semi-biographical work about the monastic deeds and miraculous exploits of a monk by the name of St. Benedict of Nursia[11]. According to early church tradition, St. Benedict lived from about 480 to 547 and is credited with the founding of Benedictine Monasticism. However, because St. Gregory did not note Benedict's exact birth and death, scholars are not certain that these dates are completely accurate. But what is clear from available sources is that St. Gregory wrote about St. Benedict in his *Second Book of Dialogues*,[12] and although it may not be considered a true biography according to modern standards, it does contain enough factual information to be considered a reliable source.

St. Gregory records that Benedict was born in Nursia, which is a village located in the mountains of northeast Rome. Benedict received a formal education in the city of Rome, but later abandoned the carnality of city dwelling, in favor of a more sanctified and solitary lifestyle. According to tradition, he lived as a hermit for a period of about three years in a place in southeast Rome, where the monk Romanus tended to him.

About that time, he was asked to be a spiritual leader by a group of monks from that region. Eventually, Benedict's strict rule and stringent leadership became too much for the undisciplined monks to bear. Therefore, they conspired to kill Benedict and attempted to poison him with a pitcher of wine. This is where Gregory recounts the first miracle God performed for Benedict. He reportedly blessed the pitcher of poisoned wine and the pitch shattered into many pieces, after which, he left the uncommited monks and began to roam the countryside of Europe. During his journeys, there were many accounts of miraculous healings and even stories of children that were raised from the dead, at the hand of St. Benedict.

According to The Modern Catholic Encyclopedia, there are thirty-eight short chapters in Gregory's book of Dialogues, which contain accounts of Benedict's life and miracles. While some chapters recount his miraculous works, "such as making water flow from rocks, sending a disciple to walk on the water, and making oil continue to flow from a flask. The miracle stories echo the events of certain prophets of Israel as well as happenings in the life of Jesus." They state that "Gregory presents Benedict as the model of a saint who flees temptation to pursue a life of attention to God."

The article continues to read, "The message is clear; Benedict's holiness mirrors the saints and prophets of old and God has not abandoned his people; he continues to bless them with holy persons." Again, according to The Modern Catholic Encyclopedia, "St. Gregory's purpose in writing about the life of St. Benedict was to edify and inspire the church of his day, and to show that saints of God, particularly St. Benedict, were still operative in the Christian Church in spite of all the political and religious chaos present in the realm. Through a balanced pattern of living and praying Benedict reached the point where he glimpsed the glory of God."

Wow! This kind of information should be particularly encouraging to charismatic believers, because it represents proof that God's charismatic grace has continued beyond the Book of Acts. That means that we have a solid foundation for the support our position of the charismatic message and ministry for today. Not only should St Benedict's stories offer encouragement for the church of St. Gregory's day, but for our day as well. And it is this kind of extra-biblical information that we may present as credible evidence, in an effort to contend for the faith and address the critics and unbelievers of our day. Just as St. Gregory used the testimony and life of St. Benedict to edify and inspire the saints of his day, so ought we to be edified, encouraged and inspired by these historic accounts.

Chapter Seven

SAME GOD...SAME GOSPEL

DIFFERENT GIFTS

Every good student of the Bible will recognize the fact that Jesus frequently used parables to convey truths about Him and the kingdom principle He taught. As we discuss the concepts and truths relative to the following topic, I believe they may best be illustrated through the use of a parable. So please bear with me as we read the following story over next few pages.

Parable of the King's Navy

There once was a very wealthy ruler who owned a shipping company. In fact, the ruler was so wealthy that he owned everything from the eastern shores of his kingdom, to as far west as the eye could see. The wealthy ruler also had a son who loved his father and loved working with his father. Soon after the son came of age, the wealthy ruler appointed his son to the royal position of Master Architect and Builder over all the land. As Master Builder, he was also commissioned to build a fleet of maritime vessels for the ruler's shipping company.

So the son began to build every kind of ship and vessel that he imagined his father might need. He built everything from the largest yachts and war ships, to the smallest rowboats and dinghies. He designed and built the fastest speedboats and the slowest tugboats. From the biggest cargo ship, to the most humble ark, he built each one with the same excellence, care and craftsmanship that he learned from his father.

Then one day a terrible storm and violent tempest wreaked havoc across the coastlands of the kingdom. It washed away many homes, businesses, and brought devastation to the inhabitants of the land. But worst of all, torrential rains and rising floodwaters washed across the kingdom coastlands and carried a host of men, women and children out to sea.

After the storm passed and the floodwaters receded, the wealthy ruler sent messengers throughout the kingdom to assess the loss and damage caused by the terrible tempest. His first order of business and highest priority was to launch a rescue mission in an effort to recover as many survivors as possible. As the wealthy ruler assembled the rescue team, he could not entrust the leadership of such an important task to just anyone, so he commissioned the only one he could trust for the position, his only son the Master Builder. Therefore he was named Commander of the Fleet by the king.

As Commander of the Fleet, the son was instructed to launch every available maritime vessel, for the oceanic rescue mission. In turn, the Commander appointed captains over thousands of ships and sent rescue parties aboard each vessel. The rescue parties were skilled in saving lives and assisting survivors. Each ship was supplied with a searchlight and a flag representing the beautiful city. The Commander instructed his captains to name their ship and raise the flag high for all to see. Then he led his fleet and teams out to sea to rescue those who were lost. As each ship encountered storm victims lost at sea, they were rescued from the cold, dark waters of death and despair and brought aboard to the protection and safety of the rescue ship.

While at sea, the Commander of the fleet was called home to begin rebuilding the beautiful city. Many survivors returned to aid in the restoration and repair of the new city. During his absence, the

Commander instructed his navy to continue the maritime mission of mercy. The captains of the fleet searched valiantly and fought courageously against enemies of the kingdom, who sought to capture and enslave lost survivors from the beautiful city.

Just as many people were about to give up all hope of being found, they looked again to see the bright beacon of searchlights shining in the distant night, offering hope for salvation and deliverance from the cold and lonely waters of death. The captains and rescue teams threw out the lifeline to save as many as were willing to come aboard each ship. No matter the size, type or name assigned to the vessel, the surviving storm victims were thankful and eternally grateful.

Finally, after completing the rebuilding of the city, the commander returned to the fleet to bring them home, to the safety of the beautiful city. The wealthy ruler and king was so overjoyed at the return of his son and the many survivors he brought back with him that he declared that day to be a day of commemoration, feasting and celebration. During the celebration, the king's son and commander of the fleet was crowned Prince of the Beautiful City! His father the king expressed his love and declared to everyone how proud he was of his faithful son. Then he expressed his love and compassion for the citizens of the Beautiful City, and for the survivors who were once lost at sea. He announced that the king would pay all of their previous debts and welcomed them to their new homes. He also rewarded each and every person for their love and courage, and for their unity and faithfulness to the king, his son and the kingdom of the Beautiful City.

What difference does it make?

By now, I'm sure that you have realized the significance of each character represented in the illustration. But for the sake of understanding, let's draw the obvious parallels. The wealthy ruler and King of course is God the Father, ruler over all of heaven and earth. The king's son who was appointed Master Architect, Builder and Commander of the Fleet is none other than our Lord and Savior Jesus Christ. He was sent by the Father to be the Savior for the world and appointed Master Builder and divine architect of the church. Through His love and forgiveness, we have been commissioned as the church, to be the fleet sent out on Christ's mission of mercy and salvation. The terrible tempest represents the devastating effects of sin upon mankind and God's beautiful creation. *"For God so loved the world that He gave His only begotten Son, that whosoever believes in Him would not perish, but have everlasting life".* (John 3:16) Therefore as we draw upon the parallels of our story, God the Father owns the fleet, Jesus is the Commander of each vessel and the

Christian flag of the Cross of Calvary is flying high atop the mast of every ship commissioned by Christ.

Now I have a few questions I ask you to consider as we glean lessons we can learn from an understanding of this parable. The first question I'd like to ask is, if the King and ruler has sent His Son on the rescue mission, and His Son, the Commander of the Fleet has launched thousands of ships to recover as many survivors as possible, then what difference does it make who the captain is of each vessel? As long as the Son has commissioned the captain and the members of the rescue party, it doesn't make a difference.

Paul addresses this issue, in 1 Corinthians the first chapter, after receiving reports of division and contentions within the church at Corinth. He begins in verse eleven where he says, *"For it has been declared to me concerning you, my brethren...that there are contentions among you. Now I say this, that each of you says, 'I am of Paul,' or 'I am of Apollos,' or 'I am of Cephas,' or 'I am of Christ."* Then he asks the question, *"Is Christ divided? Was Paul crucified for you? Or were you baptized in the name of Paul?"* (1 Corinthians 1:11-13) He then continues in chapter three to ask, *"For when one say, 'I am of Paul,' and another says, 'I am of Apollos,' are you not carnal? Who then is Paul, and who is Apollos, but ministers through whom you believed, as the Lord gave to each one?"* (1 Corinthians 3:4&5)

Paul encourages and instructs them saying, *"Now I plead with you, brethren, by the name of our Lord Jesus Christ, that you all speak the same thing, and that there be no divisions among you, but that you be perfectly joined together in the same mind and in the same judgment."* (1Corinthians 1:10) *"For we are God's fellow workers; you are God's field, you are God's building. Therefore let no one boast in men. For all things are yours: weather Paul or Apollos or Cephas ...all thing are yours. And you are Christ's, and Christ is God's."* (1Corinthian 3:9&21-23)

My next question is what difference does it make what name appeared on the side of each ship, or what it was called by the captain of the vessel, as long as the people in need of rescue did not miss the boat? Weather it was christened the S.S. Baptist, the S.S. Methodist, or if it was called Charismatic or Lutheran, does it really matter? It does not matter where folks find safety in salvation, as long as God ordains it, Jesus leads the charge and the Holy Spirit is at the helm. Our job is to throw out the lifeline of salvation, to help pull them into the safety of the Ark of Salvation, no matter what the ship is called. Now Jesus said in Matthew 4:19, *"Follow me and I will make you fishers of men."* The fact is that all around us there are men, women and children who are drowning in the oceans and seas of sin. God has sent us out into the world, as individuals and corporate bodies, to take them the good news of salvation and deliverance through His Son.

Let's look at a passage found in the gospel of Mark where Jesus responds to His disciples about this very subject. In the passage Jesus says, *"Whoever receives one of these little children in My name receives Me; and whoever receives Me, receives...Him who sent Me."* Then one of His disciples said, *"Teacher, we saw someone who does not follow us casting out demons in Your name, and we forbade him because he does not follow us."* Jesus instructs His disciples not to forbid such miracles and gives them the simple reason for His instruction. In verse forty Jesus says, *"For he who is not against me is on our side."* (Mark 9:40)

This is the simple truth that many zealous apologetic teachers seem to overlook and fail to acknowledge. They fail to recognize that we are all on the same team and in the same business of fishing for the souls of men. Instead, they engage in un-Christian and unloving criticism of charismatic Christian ministries and churches. Some even try to discourage interest in attending charismatic churches and redirecting seekers and new believers away from Word of Faith ministries. But Jesus is saying today, just as He did yesterday, *"Do not forbid them …for he who is not against Me is on our side."*

Therefore, if you have received forgiveness of sins through His blood that was shed for you and me, and you have trusted Him for your salvation; then we are on the same team. Ephesians 4:4 tells us to *"Endeavor to keep the unity of the Spirit."* What Spirit? It is the Spirit of Christ, or the Holy Spirit. Then the passage continues to tell us how, it says, *"in the bond of peace."* Please consider that it is not through the efforts of skilled apologetic debate, that we are to maintain the unity; but rather by actively choosing to participate in the bond of peace through the power of the Spirit. This means that we must make a conscious choice to put away doctrinal differences and petty schisms over secondary issues.

Ok now, what exactly is it the "bond of peace" that binds us together? It is the *"oneness"* every believer shares in Christ! Paul goes on to declare in the passage, *"There is one body and one spirit"* and that we are called, *"in one hope of our calling"*. Finally, in verse five he sums up the reason for our common bond. He says that there is, "…one Lord, one faith, one baptism; one God and Father of all, who is above all, and through all, and in you all." This brings me to my last question.

Does it really make a difference what kind of ship it is or what it was designed to do? Remember, according to the parable, the son designed and built every kind of vessel he imagined his father might need. Well as the Master Builder, Jesus has created and commissioned each and every part of the body to operate according to a specific design and purpose. Therefore, it does not matter what kind of boat He's made you to be; what matters is that we operate in the way in which we were designed. It does not matter that our specific talents, gifts and areas of ministry may differ. We are all on the same mission and called according to the same purpose.

It is from this position of unity that Paul begins to address the issues of difference and individuality. In Ephesians 4:7 he says, ***"But to each one of us, grace was given according to the measure of Christ's gift."*** Now to whom was this grace given? To each one of us! And who are we? We are the individual and corporate members of the body of Christ. What have we been given? We have been granted God's grace and ability. To what degree have we received this grace? It is according to the measure and full amount that Christ has given to each member.

Well, what's the purpose for these different gifts? According to Paul's instruction, the purpose is, ***"for equipping the saints for the work of the ministry"***, and ***"for the edifying of the body of Christ."*** (Ephesians 4:12) Let's examine these two purposes for which we are to use our different gifts. The first purpose mentioned is, ***"the perfecting of the saints for the work of the ministry."*** The word perfect in this passage refers to the maturing process of Christian growth in the life of the believer. It also refers to equipping the saints to do the work of the ministry.

What is the ministry? Ministry simply means service or to serve. Who are we to serve? We are serving God the Father by participating in the service of our Lord and Savior, Jesus Christ, through acts of worship and obedience. Now with obedience comes work. And what is the work? It is nothing less than the Great Commission. We have been instructed by the Lord Jesus to *"Go therefore and make disciples of all the nations, baptizing them in the name of the Father, and of the Son and of the Holy Spirit."* (Matthew 28: 19) Again, Jesus told His disciples to follow Him and He would make them fishermen of men.

The work of the ministry is the proclamation of the gospel of Christ and the expansion of the kingdom of heaven. Therefore, part of the purpose of the gifts and their respective diversity, is to assist the process of Christian maturity, by equipping members of the body of Christ to continue the work that was started by Jesus. We are to use our gifts to help bring people to Christ. It is for this purpose and end that the five-fold ministry and the gifts of the Spirit exist.

The second purpose is very different, but equally important. It is for the edifying, or building up, of the body of Christ. You see, once people have become part of the body, they must be fed, nourished, encouraged, strengthened and supported. This too, is where we are to use our gift, whatever it may be. We are employed as tools, for use by the Master Builder and Architect of the church, as He uses various kinds of instruments to build His church. Collectively, we are grouped in teams of ministry tools and called to the service of building the church, by utilizing our various gifts, talents and abilities.

So you see within Christendom, God has called the charismatic non-denominational church, as well as its denominationally affiliated counterparts, to be the vessels He uses to group each and every team of kingdom fishermen. Likewise, weather traditional or charismatic, we have been called and chosen by God as citizens of Zion, to help build the kingdom of heaven. We are all workers together, united for the common good and goal of glorifying God, through Jesus Christ our Lord. Amen.

Chapter Eight
ORTHODOX OR HERESY

In an effort to gain a better understanding of our role and responsibility in the Church, and to establish a solid foundation for the importance of truth in the charismatic community, let's begin with a few basic definitions. First and for most, we must start with a good understanding of what it is we are seeking. That would be nothing less than truth. According to Thorndike-Barnhart's dictionary[13], **truth** is defined as "**3** *a fixed or established principle, law, or the like; proven doctrine; verified hypothesis.*" It is also defined as "**4** *that which is true, real, or actual, in a general or abstract sense; reality: as in to find truth in God.*" I particularly like definition **6**, which simply defines truth as *"God."*

These definitions are quite consistent with the teachings of scripture. David declares in Psalm 51:6, "Behold, You desire truth in the inward parts," and in the New Testament book of John, Jesus tells us that the hour has come "…when the true worshipers will worship the Father in spirit and in truth; God is spirit and those who worship Him must worship in spirit and in truth." Then Jesus prays to the Father saying, ***"Sanctify them by Your truth. Thy word is truth."*** (John 17:17) Therefore, as believers it is of the utmost importance that we seek to know and understand God's truth in every area. In our quest to find truth, we will ultimately find God.

Next, let us consider what it means to be orthodox. **Orthodox** is defined as *generally accepted, or having generally accepted views or opinions, especially in religion.* And **orthodoxy** is the holding of correct or generally accepted beliefs; orthodox practices, especially in religion. However, I believe it is important to note that all views considered orthodox by the Church, have not always proven to be truth. From the practice of indulgences to the Church's position on Galileo's astronomical discoveries, church history is full of inconsistencies between truth and orthodox views. But eventually, all truth will become orthodox, because God reveals Himself for all to see.

Finally, I would like to submit the following definitions for your consideration of the word heresy. Again, Thorndike-Barnhart defines **heresy** as "**1** *a belief different from the accepted belief of a church, school, profession or other group."* This is the perfect definition to begin with. But let's consider another source of reference. According to The New Book of Knowledge Dictionary, **heresy** is defined as, *"An opinion or doctrine at variance with established religious beliefs; especially, dissension from or denial of Roman Catholic dogma by a professed believer or baptized church member."*

New Testament references to this word come from the Greek word *hairesis*, which denotes "a choosing, choice"; from *haireomai,* "to choose"[14]. According to Vine's Dictionary, the word came to mean "a sect" that leads to divisions. This is particularly interesting as it pertains to early Church history and the teachings that lead to changes in our understanding of truth from God's word. One case in point is the period of the Reformation.

About a hundred years before the Reformation, there were individuals who began to question the teachings and practices of the established Roman Catholic Church. Men like John Wycliffe (1324-84) who attended Oxford and was appalled because there were only five Bibles in the entire seminary. John Wycliffe made a stand by translating the Bible from Latin into English. The beauty of his translation was in its simplicity. It brought increased readability, and clarity, which made the scriptures easier for common Christians understand. Speaking of the Roman Catholic clergy of his day, Wycliffe said, "This wicked kindred wulde that the gospel slept."[15] Indeed, the Church had no intention of relinquishing it's monopoly of the faith. And any such English translated reproductions were forbidden by the Church in 1407. Therefore, he dared to challenge the practice of the Church that withheld the Holy Scriptures from the masses because it believed that divine scripture was too holy for common people.

However, as noted by a leading observer of his day, John Wycliffe's translation made the Holy Scriptures "property of the masses." He also urged the Church of his day to return to the simple life of faith of the first Christian centuries. For this, the Church leaders responded by declaring him a heretic at the Council of Constance (1414-18). Although Wycliffe had been dead for over thirty years, the council ordered his body to be dug up and the remains burned.

Another forerunner of the Reformation was William Tyndell who, like Wycliffe, wanted to translate the Bible into the common vernacular of the people. He urged the theologians of the day not to engage in scholasticism, but to return to the text of scripture rather than the commentary of men. He stressed the God given duty of the church to make the message of salvation relevant and understandable for the peasant and priest alike. However, Tyndell was also labeled a heretic, condemned to death and burned at the stake. And let's not forget John Huss of Bohemia (1369-1416), who called for more individual freedom within the Church and less rigid authoritarian control by the priest. Again, the Council of Constance decided against Huss and ordered him to be burned at the stake as well.

We can't help but ask why these men were persecuted and punished? What cardinal sin did they commit? In each case, these individuals were convicted of heresy because their views were not considered orthodox teachings of the established Church. To put it plainly, their only crime was that they tried to encourage the Church to return to the word of God! For this reason, they were sentenced to death and their teachings were declared unorthodox and heretical by the Roman Catholic establishment. However, their witness and death did not go unnoticed because they became the inspiration for Martin Luther, the Reformation and the entire Protestant Movement.

Another source of inspiration for Martin Luther was the Apostle Paul. Luther directly attributes his revelation of salvation by faith through grace to the New Testament Pauline epistles. Consider the passage from the book of Romans where Paul builds the case for Jesus as the second Adam. Such teaching would surely have been declared unorthodox and out of context by the Jewish leaders of his day.

Let us also consider the example we have in Acts where Paul argues against the need for circumcision for new gentile converts. Paul's position on this issue was clearly met with opposition by the established religious community. It was because of his revelation about Old Testament scriptures applied to a New Testament Messiah that got him in trouble, kept him in prison, and ultimately condemned him to death. When we consider this fact, many of the apologetic teachers in Paul's day regarded his teachings as unorthodox and heretical. Furthermore, I believe the irony is, had many of our modern apologetic teachers been alive in the first century, they too would have argued against the revolutionary truths and divine revelations that Paul preached to the early church. This is extremely relevant for the Charismatic Movement because from its inception, the Word of Faith message has been regarded as unorthodox, and rejected by the established Evangelical theological community. From the very beginning, it has been met with opposition and criticism, just like the early Christian Church.

My comparison to Luther continues, for he too was condemned by the established Church of his day. And just as he was condemned, so it is for the men and women of the Charismatic and Word of Faith movement of today. Just as the orthodox clergy received Luther's revelation of God's grace with controversy and skepticism, so it has been for the revelation of faith in our time. Word of Faith preachers and teachers have been criticized and to some degree ostracized, by many mainline traditional theologians, just as Luther was by the theological elite of his day.

The good news is that there is light at the end of the proverbial tunnel. All one has to do is to look at the historical record of the Church, after the Reformation, to see how God has validated and vindicated the message and memory of Martin Luther. In fact, the message of grace through faith in Christ alone that was rejected by Catholicism for hundreds of years, finally achieved its initial objective. In recent years, the Catholic Church announced that it had adopted a new position, specifically designed to include Luther's teachings on salvation by grace through faith in Christ alone.

This should be particularly encouraging and comforting to both Reformed and Charismatic believers alike! For it is a perfect testimony of the faithfulness and trustworthiness of the one who has called us. After all, the truth of God's word is universal and timeless. It will always stand against the winds of criticism and unbelief. I believe that the charismatic community can find hope and reassurance in the testimony of this truth. Therefore, we must continue to preach the revelation of faith entrusted to us by the truth of God's word, in spite of any and all opposition we encounter.

Orthodox Theological Error

While on the subject, I'd like to point out at times Martin Luther subscribed to some pretty unorthodox, unbiblical and erroneous views that are still considered bad theology today. His teaching on subjects such as marriage and polygamy are one example of error based upon his view of scripture. Another example of Luther's mistaken theological positions, which led to error, was his teachings regarding God's chosen people. His teachings cast a decidedly unfavorable shadow upon the Jewish nation because of their involvement in the crucifixion and the death of Christ.

Luther's teachings on this subject had the potential to create very negative and strongly anti-Semitic feelings and viewpoints. In fact, the affects of those teachings would prove to be so dangerous, that they helped to contribute to certain ungodly beliefs, which ultimately spawned two very ungodly offspring. They were the rise of Adolph Hitler's Nazi regime, and the development of a doctrine known as Replacement Theology, which teaches that the church has replaced the Jewish nation as the chosen people of God.

By now, I'm sure that many of you are asking, "What's the point of even mentioning Luther's past theological errors?" While others are shouting, "That's not really necessary!" So let me say that it is not my intent to belittle the memory of Martin Luther in any way. On the contrary! Luther is not remembered because of his theological errors, but rather for his contribution to the Church and his efforts to advance the Christian faith. Although, it appears that in some evangelical circles, Luther has almost been elevated to a position just below Christ as the Patron Saint of Grace through Faith.

The point I wish to make is that Martin Luther is recognized and respected for his willingness to be used by God to start a movement that helped to shape the Church of his day. So it should be for modern day charismatic men and women of God in the Word of Faith and Charismatic Movement who have given their lives for the cause of Christ. Men like Brother Kenneth Hagan Sr., who taught us that, "Now faith is the substance of things hoped for and the evidence of things not seen." He taught us to believe God for healing in our body, soul and spirit. Let's consider Pastor Chuck Smith who was probably one of the first contemporary, nondenominational pastors of the early 1960s. Men like him opened their arms in love to start

Bible studies, which became ministries that evolved into churches with open doors of acceptance. Particularly, when the doors of traditional churches were closed to newly converted, longhaired and bare foot Christian hippies.

And let us not forget about Reverend Herald Bredeson, who entered the ministry as a traditional Lutheran minister, but was transformed after being filled the Holy Spirit, after which he began to speak in tongues. Among Charismatic and Evangelical believers alike, he is remembered as one of the most influential Christian ministers of our time. His list of accomplishments and contributions to the body of Christ are extraordinary, to say the least. And yet there are still those, within the evangelical community who wish to dismiss and discredit the authenticity of his ministry gifts, service and love.

You see, such men have also helped to start a divinely inspired, God given movement. Therefore, they should be appreciated and remembered in the light of God's Hall of Faith, just like Martin Luther. Rather than the attention that they receive that has been solely focused on errors in their theological teaching.

Error of Emphasis

Please understand that I am not trying to paint a perfect picture of life and ministry in the charismatic community. Truth be told, we are certainly not without our own areas of sin and error. In fact, one of the greatest challenges we must face as a community is the **sin of over emphasizing** specific doctrines and teachings, relative to the Word of Faith message. Not that we no longer preach Christ, and Him crucified, we still do. But the first works He gave to us, we no longer teach and emphasize the way we should.

Doctrines like, *"The Power of the Prayer of Agreement"* and *"The Authority of the Believer"* as an *"Ambassador for Christ."* These are some phrases you just don't hear as much. At one time it was common to hear a message on how the prayer of faith will save the sick and the Lord will raise them up! And good teaching about how and why we should take on the whole armor of God, from which, the very identity of the movement was born in taking the shield of Faith, could always be heard. One can't help but wonder how we have drifted so far as a movement. I believe it is because we've left our first love.

Slowly, the emphasis began to shift from, ***"Seek ye first the kingdom of Heaven and all of its righteousness"*** to ***"All these things will be added unto you."*** We went from preaching, ***"Set your affection on things above;"*** to ***"Confessions in the earth realm."*** Our focus shifted from... the prayer of faith shall save the sick and the Lord shall raise them up. To confessing we are healed. In essence, we shifted the emphasis from what the word says, to what we wanted to say from the word. Consequently we are no long known for the *Message of Faith*, but rather unfortunately, we have become infamously known for the *Prosperity Message*. It's because we began to focus too much on the natural, and not enough on the spiritual.

Although this transgression is not specific to the charismatic community alone, it is however highly visible on the theological radar, because of the increased accessibility and popularity of Christian media and technology that the Charismatic Church utilizes. Consider the fact that one hundred years ago, if a preacher or teacher in a small congregation began to embrace and promote a potentially dangerous doctrine, it was not as widely known because of the sheer limitations of his presence. Even if the pastor or parishioner of a large Evangelical denomination taught something different than what was held as traditional doctrine within the church, his sphere of influence was still very limited in comparison to today. Given enough time and persistence, the influential teaching of such individuals eventually reached the ears of prominent orthodox leaders, who then spoke out against what they perceived as incorrect or heretical teaching.

In Today's church, with the aid of technologies such as global satellite uplinks and simultaneous broadcasting, Internet web casting, and even pc desktop publishing, the ability to reach and influence an audience has literally become instantaneous and worldwide in both ability and scope. Therefore, it is necessary for leaders of the Church to be extremely vigilant in their efforts to guard against erroneous and potential apostate teaching.

Herein lies the task of our prominent leaders within the Word of Faith and charismatic community! It is ever so necessary and important that you become more vigilant and vocal about the dangers and sinfulness of over emphasizing certain teachings to the degree that they become focal points, which are elevated above and beyond God's original intent and purpose. According to the word of God, such teachings are considered heresy.

Heresy of Wealth an Error of Extreme

Lately, a great deal of attention has been called to the charismatic community because of certain high profile preachers and teachers who have taken the original message of prosperity to an extreme. A recent article featured on the cover of TIME Magazine[16] asked the question, "Does God Want You to be Rich?" With this caption superimposed upon a picture of a very expensive automobile in the foreground with a cross as the hood ornament, the magazine cover captured the message of wealth in a glance.

This is certainly not the message that was taught by charismatic preachers and teachers in the early days of the movement. The Prosperity message includes all the blessings that Christ has promised us in this life; but especially the riches and rewards He has promised His people in the eternal life to come. The Prosperity Message was always part of the over all Word of Faith teaching, but during this era, we have elevated and emphasized prosperity above the balanced message of faith we once taught. This was the second sin that lead to error. (The first was pride from knowledge of the word.)

The message of prosperity is still a valuable teaching for the church today, but it should not continue to be over emphasized to the point of deception and detriment to the body of Christ. It must be balanced by the understanding that there is pain and suffering in this life, especially for the Christian who chooses to give up everything to follow Christ. This is just one example of the kind of teachings that have run-a-muck within the charismatic community and it's about time that we address these issues before it's too late.

Another example of just such an extreme was discussed during my interview with Minister Virginia Martin. Toward the end of our conversation, I asked if she had any negative experiences or issues that had caused concerns about the Word of Faith movement. With out hesitation, her immediately response was, "The extremes! Because a lot of people went overboard." She continued by saying, "A lot of people said that they had faith for something, then they got into extreme, exorbitant debt, because instead of using faith, they got into presumption."

As she began to recall memories of individuals she knew, she continued by saying, "At one time Fred Price wrote a book called *Faith, Foolishness or Presumption*. There were a lot of us who moved out of faith into presumption. And that became foolishness, because we were doing stuff that was foolish! People were going out and buying cars and saying God opened the door and gave them a car. Then they said, 'If God gave me this car, then I'm supposed to have this car,' but they didn't have a job. Therefore, they were in debt for the next five to ten years, because they had to pay for a car that they didn't have. Because you know they (the finance company) did repossess the car!

So we went from faith to presumptuousness, because we presumed God was goanna make money fall out of heaven, for us to get this car. Or somebody was going to come and hand us ten thousand dollars to make the note. That's presumptuousness! That was not faith, nor was it wisdom. So wisdom got lost in the mix and people were into presumptuousness, because they wanted to "Name it and claim it." And we were taught to *'name it'* and *'claim it'*! And there are promises of God that you can claim for your own. But they took it too far! So that was a negative (aspect) and it started to turn people away.

Then, because the people had no real foundation, when it got over into healing…if somebody in your family died, then they (Word-Faith believers) told you that they (the deceased family member) wasn't in faith. And it was as though it wasn't appointed to man once to die. You can say anything you want, but we're all goanna get out of here! It's just that simple. And God does heal, but you can't dictate when the healing comes. But what you do is stand in faith, believing that God will do what needs to be done. You are asking for healing and you believe God for healing because God is a healer. That's the premise! You believe Him for healing because He is a Healer.

If He chooses not to heal, in the way you wanted Him to at that time, then you can't say that God did not honor His word." By now, I couldn't help but interrupt. "That's right! Because He is still Sovereign" I quickly affirmed. And just as quickly, she continued, "And He may have healed, but it may not be healing as **you…**

dictated it to be! So again, those were some of the areas where people took it to far."

After our conversation, I couldn't help but appreciate the candor and concern that Sister Virginia expressed, as she shared her experiences and observations regarding this matter. Her examples reflect the negative consequences that extreme and unbalanced teaching has had upon weaker members of the body of Christ. Therefore, I wish to reiterate to stress the point.

If we, as members of the charismatic Christian community, want to return to a position of balance and credibility within the Church, we must understand one thing. We must realize that over emphasis eventually leads to error! Therefore we must begin again to place the emphasis upon the redemptive work of Christ, and the true riches available through His death, burial and resurrection. Only then can we hope to repair and restore some of the credibility we've lost, thereby bringing healing to those who have been affected by our misguided messages. The Bible says, *"If we confess our sins, He is faithful and just to forgive our sins, and cleanse us from all unrighteousness."* (1 John 1: 9)

It is most certainly consistent with the teaching of scripture, to broaden the focus even as Paul did, to include all of the blessing, riches and privileges available to us through the heavenly inheritance in Christ Jesus; both in this life and in the world to come. So then, I am convinced that by God's grace, we can be both orthodox Christians and a charismatic Christians as well. In fact, that would make us orthodox-charismatic believers. Wow! Talk about a new creation in Christ Jesus, how cool is that?

✝
Chapter Nine
COMPROMISE of CREDIBILTY

Prosperity Propaganda

As the mid 80's and the early 90s progressed, that era of time gave rise to the Me generation. A generation which defined itself with terms associated with success, such as the yuppies (Young Urban Professionals) who would do just about anything to climb the corporate ladder, just to get an office with their name on the door and a window with a view. This kind of success driven mentality began to fuel a cultural revolution marked by iconic business personalities and idolized sports figures alike. No longer did the word "others" mean very much, but rather, the term "personal" became the buzzword of the day. From personal computers, to personal portfolio and wealth building opportunities, to the simple pursuit of personal health, wealth and happiness that was the theme of the day. I believe this is where we began to slip.

So where did we miss the mark? One can't help but wonder how we have drifted so far as a movement. I believe that some were along the way we bought into the propaganda of the culture and lost sight of the real message. We began to follow the spirit of the culture, rather than the spirit of God. According to scripture, believers ought not to be led astray, by teachers who preach false doctrines that fail to focus on Christ and His teachings. Jesus said in Matthew 6:24 that Christians cannot love God and also love money. Therefore, our affection and focus must be on God rather than the opportunity for riches and wealth.

I remember all too well, the days when I could go into a worship service that had begun before my arrival and I could literally feel the hair stand up on the back of my neck, as the presence of God filled the room. An immediate and overwhelming desire to worship would come upon me as all other thoughts regarding people and activities quickly fled my minds eye. It was in that kind of setting that I personally witnessed some of the most miraculous moves of the God and heard some of the most profoundly inspired and insightful messages.

But that was then and this is now. And now, there has been a definitive change in the over all climate of ministry within the Word of Faith movement. I believe that it has been a change for the worse marked by a loss of credibility as well as a loss of God's presence and demonstrative power in ministry. My fear is that if this trend continues and is left unchecked, then the very existence of a charismatic presence in future end-time ministry may hang in the balance.

If we hope to reverse this trend, we must begin to ask what happened and why did things change so drastically? To help us get a handle on the gravity of this issue and the pervasiveness of the problem, I wanted to talk to someone who has had first hand experience in dealing with the charismatic community in this area. Therefore, I called upon the assistance of my teacher and friend, Dr. Conny Williams Th. D.

Dr. Conny is a Dean and Administrator for the International College of Bible Theology. She was originally born and raised in the beautiful city of Frankfort, Germany, and came to America in 1983. After receiving Christ as Lord and Savior, she attended the International College of Bible Theology and Midwest Theological Seminary, where she received her Doctorate. Later on, she was asked to accept a new position as the Dean and Administrator of the I.C.B.T. satellite branch in St. Louis. She holds a Ph.D. in Theological Studies.

One evening after class, I told Dr. Conny about my effort to write a book and asked if I could get an interview, she agreed and later gave me a phone call to set a date and time for my wife and I to come over. We chose the next available weekend for the interview. Of course as fate would have it, on the day before our meeting, a winter storm brought snow and bad weather conditions. However, despite the weather alert and travel advisory, we were at her door the following Saturday by 2:00 pm. She welcomed us with a warm greeting and a hot cup of authentic German coffee.

After we sat for a spell to enjoy her hospitality and the warmth and comfort of her festively decorated home, I didn't know exactly how much time we might have, so I jumped right in and began asking a few questions about her ministry to the charismatic community. During our two-hour conversation, I asked Dr. Conny what her thoughts were regarding the recent headline scandals and compromising behavior of some high profile charismatic ministers. What she had to say was interesting and insightful to say the least, as she talked about several major factors that have contributed to a loss of credibility in the charismatic community.

Compromise of Truth

At the end of our last chapter, Minister Virginia Martin eluded to the very reason for the compromise of credibility that has changed the face of charismatic ministry. She said people began to leave the charismatic community because of extreme teachings that "took it too far." The result was mass disaffiliation. Many people returned to their former denominational churches, while others left the Church all together. The sad part is, when they left, they were disappointed, discouraged and disillusioned by the Word of Faith message.

It's not that they stopped preaching the truth about the redemptive work of Christ and the cross of Calvary. Nor did they cease to preach the importance of God's grace with regard to salvation. The problem was that many of the leaders who were most visible within the Charismatic community began to preach a doctrine of faith, prosperity and healing that was no longer balanced by the truth of God's word. The focus was no longer on God, but on man; it was no longer centered on the gift-Giver, but rather on the gifts. It was no longer centered on Christ, but on Christians.

During my interview with Dr. Conny Williams, I mentioned the comments that Minister Martin made about compromised teaching and its affects upon the Word of Faith community. Dr.

Conny agreed that the compromise of truth was the first factor that contributed to the initial loss of credibility.

Fun in the Son on the Charismatic Beach

To best illustrate the point that Dr. Conny wished to make, she began by sharing a dream that God had given her about the Charismatic Church in its beginning. As she leaned forward on the couch, she began by saying, "One night I had a dream. In this dream, I am on the beach. And I have a little girl in front of me and I'm braiding the little girl's hair. Everybody is la-de -doddering around, having fun, because that's what you're supposed to do on the beach. And I was braiding the little girl's hair and I was making money doing that.

And then the Lord said, 'Well, you're having a good time now turn around.' And I turned around and behind me were mountains. And they looked very dangerous because they were wooded mountains (dark forest). And there was a very dark cloud on top of that mountain. And I saw somebody walk into those trees on top of the mountain. Then the Lord spoke to me and said, "While you are having a good time down here, he is walking up there in danger." He was way on top and he was walking on dangerous ground."

Dr. Conny's dream about life on the "charismatic beach" is

significant on many levels. First of all it illustrates the attitude of many charismatic Christians, who believe that the Christian life should be nothing but fun in the sun. They are like children, interested only in playing on the beach, enjoying the beauty and benefits of the gifts while unconcerned and uninterested in the possibility of peril, pain and suffering.

And while there are those who are on the beach who are more mature and do provide care for others on the beach, the care that they provide is primarily for the outward adorning (such as the braiding of hair) for which they desire financial compensation for the care they provide. In fact, we are so preoccupied with life on the beach that we fail to look around to see that the Christian life is not just a party on the beach. There is an entirely different level and environment in the spirit that God is calling our attention to.

She said, "In the beginning of the Charismatic Movement, it was a move of God, because it freed us who were bound by tradition. It freed me... it set me free! But we took that freedom and left out the depth of God. But God really wanted us to take His depths and combine His freedom. Now that is power!

That is why I like the title of one of your chapters about orthodoxy (Orthodoxy or Heresy). Because if someone were to ask me (what kind of Christian I am), I'm an orthodox Christian, but I am also a Charismatic. I can be an orthodox (Christian) because I believe in the fundamentals, I believe the word of God is the final authority…I believe that you can move mountains with a little bit of faith. I believe that! But at the same time, we got excited about God, but we (only) wanted to keep the excitement. We didn't want to combine the foundation that we had with the new thing, the new wave that God was bringing in. The refreshing and the new anointing God was bringing in. We didn't want to combine it; we just threw everything to the dogs and ran after the Charismatic Movement, and went buck wild with it."

"So that's my dilemma with the Charismatic Movement." said Dr. Conny, "We've become flaky in our teaching and we give the kind of messages that the people want to hear. The word of God tells us that in the last days, the people will not endure sound doctrine. There is nothing wrong with the move of God. There is nothing wrong with people being excited about God and there's nothing wrong with people being blessed. But if that become the motivating force, then there is a problem."

What Dr. Conny said was right on, because at that point, we exchange truth for a lies that titillate our itching ears. Therefore, the first steps in our efforts to return to a position of credibility within the community of faith, is to repent of the sin of error and begin once again to preach and teach the pure, unadulterated word of God, without compromising its truth. This is imperative if we hope to be instrumental in God's end-time message and ministry.

Personality Centered Ministries

Another factor that I believe contributed to a loss of credibility for charismatic preachers and teachers was a shift from Christ centered ministries to personality driven ministries within the charismatic community. In a previous chapter, I mentioned that in the early days of the Charismatic Movement, pastors, preachers and teachers were not apt to refer to themselves with any form of title or prestige. But slowly, the humility that was once a signature characteristic of our leaders began to change. As the popularity and prosperity of certain ministers increased, so did their prestige and notoriety in ministry. As a result, many well know speakers within the charismatic community became household names not only in the church, but also among the who's-who of secular society as well.

Again, this is where we have missed the boat and got off of the beaten path. Jesus said, "If I be lifted up, I will draw all men unto me."(John 12:32) God has also said that He will not share His glory with any man. And now many of our prominent preachers and big-name teachers have fallen into the sin of pride, greed, infidelity and a host of other forms of ungodliness.

Compromise of Humility

As we discussed the change in pulpit demeanor of certain ministers that we have noticed, we agreed that those ministers are very different from the way they began. I noted that there is a lot of arrogance that we see that comes across the pulpit now that you did not see before. And there was sincerity and humility that was present in the early days that is no longer present today. This discussion prompted Dr. Conny's second reason for a compromise of credibility, which was a loss of humility. This second reason for the problem was the nonverbal message that was communicated across the pulpit, from the leaders of the Charismatic Movement. It was an attitude of arrogance that said, "Look at me! I'm a celebrity and a superstar!"

I began by asking what she felt about comments that have been made about the way that many charismatic ministers come across when ministering from the pulpit. I then reminded her about a comment she had made about superstars becoming falling stars, which prompted her response by saying; "The Charismatic Movement has become a Hollywood religion because we are on T.V. now, which before that, there was not much religion on television. Now that we are on TV, not only are we on TV, we are trying to measure up to Hollywood standards! Now, these days if you look into the pulpit and now that the Hollywood stardom is out there, it's a desire of many because it seems that you are really not anybody unless you are on TV."

Dr. Conny continued with an example of the kind of impact that this phenomena is having upon ministers with smaller ministries throughout the charismatic community. She recalled that she was flicking through channels one day while preparing to leave for church, she came across a local minister who caught her attention. She said, "I wonder who that is? It was some guy from Bellville (Illinois) who was preaching. As he began to preach, with his motions and his words, I see Noel Jones all over him. I mean his mannerisms were just like Noel Jones! I began to laugh aloud and said 'He looks just like Noel Jones!' That's what caught my attention. And as I was sitting there laughing, I thought, why can't you just be yourself?"

She then said that she continued to listen to that local charismatic preacher, but noticed a lack of content and depth within his message. "You noticed that he wasn't at the depth of Noel Jones because he started talking about (things like), 'You women ought to want to look anointed.' And I thought to myself, how do you look anointed? Tell me how you do that because I don't understand." As we chuckled about her response, she continued by saying, "I knew that he was trying to be the superstar preacher by the thing he was doing with his hands (Noel has this thing he does with his hands), and he used a few big words, but the depth of his message was flaky. There was no substance to it...none what so ever!"

"So today what you see is we fashion ourselves after what we think is something big, or what we see in someone else, instead of being the best you can be...which is, "You!" She then emphasized the fact that while this may be especially true among men, women in charismatic ministries are just as guilty because everybody wants to be a Paula White or Juanita Bynum.

At this point, I interjected to comment on the very issue that Dr. Conny had just raised. I mentioned the fact that I have noticed something that I have identified as a "disconnect" between the experience portrayed on television, and the experience of the common everyday charismatic local ministry. There is a real disconnect between what we see in the glorified reality of Christian television ministries, as apposed to the reality we see in the small charismatic churches across America. But at the same time, we also see many ministers within these churches trying to emulate what they see in superstar personality ministries, as if it were real.

She responded immediately by saying, "We've lost power! And the power is associated directly with humility! It is directly associated," she reiterated with even greater emphasis. This insightful observation struck a cord of truth in us that caused my wife and I to respond with a resounding "Amen." She then said, "Go to the days when people did get up from the dead. Remember the places and ministries where people were rolled in on gurneys, taking their last breath, and they got up (after they received healing) and ran out. Those ministries were involved in humility. It wasn't about big money …there was no money! This is exactly the kind of definitive change, mentioned earlier, that I was talking about. At one time, you could take someone to a charismatic service, and you could expect God to touch that individual and do something wonderful. Unfortunately, this is no longer the case because of the compromise of humility. In fact, this may be the greatest problem and loudest message still with us today.

Compromise of Continuity

During the interview with Pastor Femi, he touched on the subject of mega-church perception and its influence upon Christianity. In the discussion, the difference between the Hollywood perception of the charismatic church and the reality of the "everyday" local charismatic church also came up. Femi said, "If you watch the media, you'd think every church is a mega church. You would think all the churches in America have two thousand, three thousand, four or five thousand people. But the average size of a church in America is a hundred and fifty people. That's an average church. Some churches have ten, some have fifteen, some have twenty or thirty people, but we can not judge the move of God by the loudest folks."

Femi continued by saying, "There was a time in church when my wife and I said 'Why does everybody have a problem with us?' because we kept hearing complaints. So we sat down and made a list of the people who were complaining. And we found out that they were less than two percent of the church. But because of the volume and the frequency, we assumed it was everybody. But it wasn't everybody! It was just a couple of people, who had particular problems that if one could put it into perspective, you could deal with it. It's like you see smoke and you assume the whole house is burning down. But the whole house is not burning down. It's just a pot on the stove. So it is the same way with the (charismatic) move in Christianity, we hear a lot of rubbish on TV, but there are a lot of people in a lot of churches who are still preaching the Word of God."

Pastor Femi ended his comments about mega churches by saying, "It's like Hollywood...Christian Hollywood. TBN is our Hollywood, you know. All those guys who come and yell, and have these churches with twenty thousand, thirty thousand, forty thousand and fifty thousand people, I'm sure that some of them are doing a really good work. But most pastors have churches with ten, fifteen, twenty, fifty or hundred to two hundred members; and they are dedicated. They are loyal to God and to the ministry. And they are committed to the people! They are praying for the people. They are not CEO Pastors…they don't have a lot of money. They don't know the seven steps to church growth, but they just love God and they are meeting the needs of the sheep. And that is all that counts in the final analysis!"

This is exactly what I meant when I referred to the "disconnect" between the version of charismatic Christianity that we see on TV, verses the reality of the charismatic Christianity that is experienced by everyday believers in the local church. It is not the truth about the charismatic church or about what goes on in charismatic churches all across the country and around the world. Not everyone is trying to "be about the bling!" That's not the true heart of most pastors I know. Therefore, I believe that the media's representation of the charismatic community is in fact a misrepresentation and it is very misleading about what the charismatic church is all like. That is again, the reason I wanted to write the book from the perspective of the everyday, charismatic Christian; from the perspective of people who are not on TV, but who are actually living everyday life in the charismatic church.

Compromise of Charismatic Counsel

Now from the Hollywood Charismatic Christian perspective, we are looking good, we're shining, we have charisma, we almost entertain, and not all of that is bad. However, that place of notoriety puts a minister that started out called and only for the cause of Christ, in a position where he has to deal with a whole lot more than just preaching the word of God. Now he or she is confronted with becoming a celebrity. They are thrust upon the stage of Hollywood fame and are preoccupied by what it takes to stay up there.

First of all, the money is outrageous! Just to stay on TV for even thirty minutes it cost an astronomical amount of money. So some ministers, out of desperation, have to ask for money at the end of their shows. That has sometimes caused many ministers to compromise their faith. Then the other thing is that because of the fame, all those things that can become weaknesses, like lust (from women throwing themselves at the men and vise-versa). That has put another pressure on the ministers, and so, in there private life they began to fall. And because they are in the limelight, it has really put a damper on the credibility of the Charismatic Movement. They are called shysters. Unsaved people say, 'They are worse than we are.' Other people say that they are just entertaining out there ...you know; things like that.

And I think there is something to be said in their defense, because those people have not been where those ministers are. However, when you know that you are way up there, and God has allowed you to get up there, you ought to have enough sense to surround yourself with people that can protect you and that can help you. They get so high that they feel they have no place to go, therefore who will counsel, who can counsel the superstar Christian?" Dr. Conny Williams then summed it all up by say that she attributes the demise of many of our most popular ministers, at least in part, to their inability to find effective counsel in times of weakness. This has caused a compromise of credibility for the charismatic minister who falls. And they do fall, because they will not seek counsel until it is too late.

In no way is this intended to imply that there is an excuse for such behavior. On the contrary, it simply underscores the tremendous need for greater character development and spiritual maturity in the lives of ministers of the gospel of Jesus Christ. It speaks to the need for attention and commitment to personal preparation in areas like integrity, humility and self-control. Such disciplines must be enforced from an internal understanding of the kind of responsibility we have as stewards of the word of God and the testimony of the gospel of Jesus Christ

If we fail to embrace and implement these kinds of principles and disciplines into the mental and spiritual mindset of Charismatic Christian life, we will find that the resulting consequence will be sobering to say the least. We have a clear picture presented to us through the parable of the faithful steward found in Luke 12:47-48, where we read of the impending outcome and judgment for those who continue in sin. It says, *"And that servant who knew his master's will, and did not prepare himself or do according to his will, shall be beaten with many stripes. But he who did not know, yet committed things deserving of stripes, shall be beaten with few."* This description applies to high profile charismatic leaders, preachers and teachers, as well as each and every pastor of a local congregation within the charismatic community. The remainder of verse forty-eight continues, *"For everyone to whom much is given, from him much will be required; and to whom much has been committed, of him they will ask the more."*

Dr. Conny said that this was the point of the dream that God showed her. "For those people who are on that level, the dangers are so much more. The danger that the man was walking in was not that he was walking in sin, but that he was walking at a level in the kingdom of God where he was in danger all the time. Not because he was a weak person, but because the enemy will come to try and get you, especially if you are anointed and especially if you are making a difference in peoples lives. That's what counts!"

Compromise of the Anointing

Another area that Dr. Conny Williams mentioned was the propensity for charismatic ministers to continue in sin because the grace of God is taken for granted. Dr. Conny said, "As we grow in the word of God and we get a real revelation of the grace of God, once you realize what the grace of God will do and you do fall, you know that you can get back up. You know that God will forgive you. You know it! It's not "maybe He would." No…you know He will. And that in it self can get you on a road where you repeatedly fall when your eyes are not kept on God; knowing that God will forgive you.

But what people don't understand is it is not a matter of will God forgive you. Of course He will forgive you. The matter is the anointing is compromised!" As I paused for a moment to digest what she had just said, I realized the truth of this statement. She quickly continued and said, "While salvation is free, and it's not going to necessarily keep you out of heaven as long as you keep repenting, but it will cost you the anointing."

This insightful observation is completely consistent with what we find in the life and ministry of individuals who continually take the grace of God for granted as they refuse to cease from the sins, which so easily beset them. And sadly, such behavior ultimately affects the entire body, resulting in a sacrifice of the anointing and a compromise of the credibility in the charismatic community.

If we ever want to see a reversal of this trend, then we must forsake and reject our preoccupation with what has been labeled as a "sloppy agape" kind of grace, and begin to seek a return to the whole counsel of God in this matter. That version of sound biblical grace tells us to "lay aside every weight and sin which does so easily beset us." Therefore we must learn to dedicate ourselves to the concept and effort of living a blameless life.

Credibility is Everything

In fact, when the Apostle Paul begins to list the requirements for the office of a bishop in 1Timothy 3:1-7, he begins with this indispensable virtue. The passage reads as follows:

> 1 *This is a faithful saying: If a man desires the position of a bishop, he desires a good work. 2 A bishop then must be blameless, the husband of one wife, temperate, sober-minded, of good behavior, hospitable, able to*

teach; 3 not given to wine, not violent, not greedy for
money, but gentle, not quarrelsome, not covetous; 4
one who rules his own house well, having his children
in submission with all reverence 5 (for if a man
does not know how to rule his own house, how will
he take care of the church of God?); 6 not a novice,
lest being puffed up with pride he fall into the same
condemnation a the devil. 7 Moreover he must have
a good testimony among those who are outside, lest
he fall into reproach and the snare of the devil.

In this passage, Paul writes to encourage and instruct young Timothy, his apprentice and protégé in the gospel. Paul begins his address with an exhortation by declaring, *"This is a faithful saying"* or to quote Amplified Bible, *"The saying is true and irrefutable: if a man eagerly seeks the office of a bishop (superintendent, overseer)"* then Paul says that man, *"desires a good work"* or *"an excellent task (work)."* This is to say, that if one desires a leadership role in the church, particularly the position of a pastor and shepherd, it is a very good thing indeed. But with that desire, there must be a truly foundational understanding of what it really means to be a leader, and what the requirements are on a personal level.

Paul's begins to instruct young Timothy in verse two (2), where he starts by saying, *"A bishop must be blameless,"* or that superintendent or overseer, *"must give no grounds for accusation but must be above reproach."* This is the area where far too many of our charismatic pastors and leadership have blown it, as they have come under the scrutiny of public ministry. In our pursuit for the blessings of happiness through health, wealth and prosperity, we have come under reproach through the deceitfulness of riches. Because of this new celebrity Christian superstar mentality that has crept in to the church, our leaders have given grounds for accusations, through a perverted prosperity message that has tainted our community with the sin of celebrity scandals. Please consider the recent investigations into the questionable financial practices of some of the biggest names in charismatic ministries. If we are completely honest about the situation, it is not an issue of assets from prosperity, but rather the issue is the liability associated with excessive wealth and extravagant lifestyle. That is why, as Christians, we have been called to a lifestyle of temperance and modesty.

Verse two continues by saying that a bishop (superintendent, overseer) is to be "the husband of one wife." This speaks to another issue that has compromised the credibility of some high profile charismatic ministers. Their inability to honor the vow and institution of marriage has brought reproach upon the charismatic Christian community of the church. It is the sin of unfaithfulness, which is expressed in the form of adultery, divorce and sexual immorality. Their stories are pasted on the covers of magazines and Internet websites all across America and even around the world.

In Isaiah 53:1, the prophet asked the question, *"Who has believed our report? And to whom has the arm of the Lord been revealed?"* As Christians, we must understand that credibility is everything when it comes to performing our job as witnesses to fulfill the great commission. If we loose our credibility, then we loose our witness. If we loose our witness, then we loose our believability. If we people can no long believe our testimony, then our ability to make disciple of Christ is compromised. And if our ability to make disciples is compromised, then the very purpose and mission of Christianity is made null and void!

The remainder of this passage simply applies to holy living that leads to credibility and good standing in the church and more importantly, in the world around us. Verse seven sums it up by saying, "Furthermore, he must have a good reputation and be well thought of by those outside [the church], lest he become involved in slander and incur reproach and fall into the devils trap. What is the devils trap? He desires to steal our witness and to destroy our testimony in the gospel. The ultimate goal is to get us to compromise our life in Christ to such a degree that we are rendered useless and ineffective in the faith. Therefore, we must begin to pray for true repentance and restoration for those pastors and leaders who have fallen short of the grace of God.

Chapter Ten
FAITH UNDER FIRE

During the early 1990's, my wife and I decided to begin our son's early childhood education, by placing him in private school. As a child, my wife had attended a private Lutheran school, of which she had many fond memories. Therefore, when the time came for us to choose the kind of school that he would attend, the choice was pretty much a no-brainer. After choosing the right school and getting to know everyone, my wife developed a friendship with the mother of one of the kids in my son's class. Soon after, she told us about a new Christian radio station, which had begun to broadcast in our area.

It was at that time, we were introduced to many of the religious, conservative radio programs, which have become influential members within mainstream conservative Christian media. For the most part, there was a great deal I appreciated about the preaching and teaching, which became available to our area. But certain other broadcasted evangelical programs really began to create an unhealthy climate among charismatic believers who listened to those programs. That's because some evangelical teachers had developed apologetic programs, from which they began to publicly criticize and denounce the teachings, doctrines and leaders associated with charismatic and Word of Faith communities.

As a matter of fact, on one occasion while driving home, I listened to the host of a popular evangelical talk-radio apologetic program, who counseled a caller about how and where to find a local church. When the new convert explained that he had come to faith in Christ while attending services at a local charismatic church, the show's host began to question the authenticity of the caller's conversion experience. Needless to say, I was utterly surprised and completely outraged by the line of questions and comments made by this Christian apologetic representative! After pressing beyond my initial aggravation, I continued to listen in disbelief, as he proceeded to discourage the caller from becoming a member of that charismatic congregation. Near the end of his conversation with the caller, the radio host was able to convince the new believer to redirect his efforts to find a local church. He did so by implying that the teaching received at charismatic churches was unorthodox and less than trustworthy.

When I began my research into the subject matter for this book, again I was surprised and honestly unprepared for what I encountered. I genuinely never expected to find the level of hostility and opposition that was so vehemently expressed by other Christians toward the Word of Faith message and the charismatic community. Admittedly, I had become accustomed to the complaints and objections raised by certain religious radio hosts and their well-educated apologetic guests. But after typing in a few keywords and phrases into an Internet search engine, all of their criticisms and complaints paled in contrast to the spirit of unbridled hostility that was revealed on every web page that followed.

I suppose that radio and its format demands a certain amount of reservation because of rules and regulations that govern the media. Therefore, comparing information broadcasted via radio, to the Internet's unrestricted information might be like comparing apples and oranges. But since I was investigating a subject matter particular to Christian interest, I never expected what can only be described as a mean spirited attack upon all things related to the Charismatic Movement.

My heart melted with disappointment, pain and grief as I read page after page of anti-charismatic rhetoric. I was also overcome with a measure of righteous indignation, which in fact, rekindled the same feelings I had when I initially heard the apologist on the radio, who ripped away at my charismatic roots. After talking with other Christians, who worship and fellowship within charismatic Christian camps, I heard the same feelings expressed by other believers. They too experienced feelings of hurt, grief, doubt and betrayal, because of the unrelenting and un-empathetic attacks upon their Christian faith.

Unfortunately, this is the kind of verbal assault that many apologetic teachers practice, when dealing with charismatic issues. They dismiss the note worthy contributions, and the good that charismatic ministries do, as they focus upon negative aspects of the movement. They play-up what they consider to be inaccurate and erroneous teaching. And they take statements that are intended to be used for the purpose of illustration, and declare them to be unsound doctrine, for the purpose of denouncing charismatic teachings, all while playing down any example of solid biblical teaching, or note worth Christian activity by Word of Faith preachers and teachers.

Some folks representing the Evangelical apologetic position even called into question the authenticity of salvation received by believers in charismatic churches.

It is for this very reason I was galvanized again, to bring a voice of compassion and representation to the debate, on behalf of this most controversial member of the body of Christ. Particularly, when defending our position against those who seek to super-impose the commandments, teachings and traditions of men upon scripture, and call it the word of God. It is at those times, that we need our preachers and teachers to vigorously defend our position in the faith with a charismatic Christian apologetic response that will silence the critics and testify to God's grace on our behalf.

Touched by an Apology

However, there is a glimmer of hope and ray of sunshine that has emerged on the ecumenical event horizon, of the evangelical apologetic community. It offers hope and healing for members of the body of Christ who have been affected by the critical fallout from the evangelical-charismatic Christian debate. It appears that God is bringing about a change in the attitude of hostility that some evangelical Christians have shown toward the charismatic community.

While on the parking lot one day at work, I was setting in the car listening to the radio during my lunch-break. There, on the same evangelical Christian radio station; I was blessed with a gift! It was a wonderful expression of love and one of the best examples of Christian compassion that I had heard in a long time. On the very same evangelic Christian apologetic program, I heard a gentleman talking to the host of the program, about the lack of compassion and the divisive nature of the attacks by some evangelical Christians that had been directed toward the charismatic community.

The gentleman mentioned the fact that he was the editor for an evangelical Christian magazine, and that he had written an article about this subject. In reference to the magazine article, he explained the need for evangelical apologetic representatives to become more sensitive to the "spirit and attitude of their presentation," when delivering the message of truth. He also emphasized the need for apologist to defend the gospel from a position of humility, rather than the attitude of arrogance that exudes from so many haughty, high-minded scholars. He went on to explain just how some evangelical apologist may have caused hurt and detrimental harm, through their zealous but unloving actions.

This was huge! At that moment, it was almost impossible to express the feelings I experienced as I listened to his apology. I was absolutely ecstatic and overjoyed! All I could do was shake my head and lift my hands in praise and thanksgiving, because that brother's confession and apology stood as a wonderful testament, to the goodness and faithfulness of the Lord our God. As I left the car to return to work, I knew without a doubt that it is God who fights our battles. He alone, through Christ Jesus, has made us excepted in the beloved. And through His spirit, we will be made one, even as He is one.

Examining Our Faith

As we continue to minister to those who are part of the charismatic community, it is important to emphasize the need to judge ourselves, so that others do not judge us. We must be careful to examine our lives, our works and our motives in the truth and light of God's word so that we may be found blameless and useful for the Master's kingdom. I believe for the most part, this is the side (the side of truth and sound doctrine), that we will be found supporting and defending, especially in the face of biblical scrutiny and critical opposition. In such cases, it is imperative that we stand together as one member, with one voice. To declare the truth and the specific revelation of that truth, which God by His grace, has given to the Charismatic community through the word of faith message.

The first steps in addressing the firestorm of criticism and controversy must be made from a heart of righteousness and humility. Therefore, we must honestly consider the criticism made by others within the body, and evaluate the legitimacy of their claims. However, if after careful examination and consideration, we find that our teachings are completely consistent with the Spirit and truth of God's holy word, then we should preach and teach such truth with the boldness and confidence that comes with a full assurance of faith!

Next, we must also deal honestly with those within our ranks, who preach and teach erroneous and unsound doctrine. When and where we find it necessary, we must be willing to examine their teachings for truth and error. Then determine if there is error; address the point and source of such error. And finally, we must be willing to confess, repent and renounce the sin of our error and begin to say what God has said about the issue. If necessary, we must also mark those preachers and teachers who choose to continue unabated, in the propagation of error.

Contending for the Faith

Let's begin by reviewing a passage of scripture found in the book of Jude, starting with verse three. *"Beloved, while I was very diligent to write to you concerning our common salvation, I found it necessary*

to write to you exhorting you to contend earnestly for the faith which was once for all delivered to the saints."

In the passage, Jude begins his address with the word Beloved. This word is a clear indicator of the spirit and position of the author's heart as he penned this letter. It suggests an out stretched arm with an open hand extended in loving concern, as it beckons to the one for which it waits; to join him as he proceeds in the direction he desires to lead God's people. It is in this same spirit of love and compassion that we must address those who oppose the charismatic position of faith. We must remember that they are family, despite their unchristian and unloving responses. Then he mentions what he calls, *"our common salvation"*. It is the commonality of our love for Christ; our faith in Christ; and the salvation that can only be received through the finished work of Christ, which we share as believers. The fact is that we are all blood-bought brothers and sisters in Christ, and we should treat one another as such.

It is this fact that we must constantly be mindful of, when addressing the differences between the many members of the body of Christ. Again, it is this fact that is often overlooked and ignored by those who so quickly and easily criticize and ostracize the Word of Faith and charismatic community. If we choose to respond in kind, then our efforts to communicate the truth of scripture and revelation from God's word become little more than a game of theological Tug-o-War or an apologetic shoving match between kingdom kids of opposing Christian camps.

Jude goes on to exhort the reader to **"contend earnestly for the faith."** Exactly what does he mean by instructing the reader to contend for the faith? The word **contend** generally means to work hard, fight or struggle against difficult; or to take part in a contest, to vie or compete; and finally, to argue or dispute. Although this definition provides us with a basic understanding, it is still incomplete in its description for this passage. The word used here in the Greek is **epagonizamai**, which signifies "to contend about a thing, as a combatant." Herein, we find both our role and response, for engaging the opposition. Then Jude adds the word "earnestly" to convey the intensity and sincerity of our effort with which we are to contend. It is to be done whole-heartedly without reservation.

Therefore, as combatants for Christ, we are to work hard in the struggle, as we earnestly fight the good fight of faith. Before engaging in the fight, we must identify our enemy. The word again tell us in Ephesians 6:12, ***"For we wrestle not against flesh and blood, but against principalities, against powers, against the rulers of the darkness of this age, against spiritual hosts of wickedness in the heavenly places. Therefore take up the whole armor of God, that*** *you may be able to withstand in the evil day, and having done all, to stand."* (Ephesians 6:12, 13) We must understand that our enemy is not our brother or sister in the faith. At best, they are sibling rivals among sons of God, competing for the same prize. At worst, they are simple pawns, allowing him or herself to be used by our true adversary. That adversary is none other than Satan himself, and his host of spiritual henchmen.

We must also remember that we share a relationship with our rivals, therefore we must respond first from a position of genuine love and compassion, with the goal of attaining the prize for which we contend. And what is the prize? It is, *"the faith which was once for all delivered to the saints."* Therein, lays the focal point of our response, when dealing with such criticism. The passage in Ephesians 6, verses fourteen and fifteen, proceed by instructing us to put on the whole armor of God. After referring to each piece of protection, the scripture says in verse sixteen, *"Above all, taking the shield of faith with which you will be able to quench all of the fiery darts of the wicked one."*

Again we can see the dual nature of the ministry of the church in the battle we face. We are not only contending against the forces of darkness, but also against misguided sibling rivalry as well. The truth is that the Word of Faith and its community of faith, is under fire, therefore we must do everything in God's power to stand against the attacks of Satan and the critical complaints from our brothers and sisters in other denominations. But what better community is there, than the Word of Faith community by virtue of its name and commission, to stand as defenders of the faith?

We have a responsibility to fight for the preservation of the faith that was originally delivered to the church, by Jesus Himself, along with all of the provisions, gifts and attributes originally ascribed to that faith. Secondly, we are to fight for the protection, strength and personal witness of faith for each and every believer for whom Christ died. Just as he is interceding on behalf of His saints, we too must intercede on behalf of our brothers and sisters in the Lord.

Faith to Fight False Teachers

To fight a good fight, everyone knows that you must develop a good battle plan. And part of the plan has to be an honest evaluation of your strengths and weaknesses, how you got to where you are, and where you want to be in the end. In the previous chapters, we have taken a look at some of the attributes and characteristics of the charismatic community that can and should be considered areas of strength. As we continue reading the next few verses from our passage in Jude, I believe that it will also help us in our process of self-evaluation to point out some major areas of vulnerability and error in the faith community.

Continuing on to verse four of Jude, the passage reads, *"For certain men have crept in un-noticed, who long ago were marked out for this condemnation, ungodly men, who turn the grace of God into lewdness and deny the only Lord God and our Lord Jesus Christ."* (Jude vs. 4) According to this passage, the first place we must begin to look is within our very own ranks. 2 Peter 2:1 also warns us about the fact that there will be false prophets among us, *"who secretly bring destructive heresies…even denying the Lord who bought them."* Verse two explains the reason we must take an active offensive stand against such teachers. It says, *"Many will follow their destructive ways."*

This is exactly why we must do everything possible to stem the tide of erroneous teaching that has become so pervasive within our ranks. We must deal with those brothers and sisters, in the charismatic community, who preach and teach extreme interpretations of charismatic doctrines. Considering the influence that mega ministries have within the body of Christ, we must be willing to confront and denounce the preachers of false teachings among us.

Think of it as an intervention for the charismatic family of believers. Especially those who are in authority within our community, they must be willing to assist in such an intervention. We have been given the pattern for intervention in Galatians 6:1. This is where our leaders and ministers must begin. However, if we fail to act, then it will ultimately lead to very negative consequences. The consequences are plainly stated in 2 Peter 2:3, *"By covetousness they will exploit you (the body) with deceptive words."*

I believe that exploitation is only the first stage of deception. In fact the unhindered results are described for us in Revelation 3:15 which says, *"Because you say, 'I am rich, have become wealthy and have need of nothing – and do not know that you are wretched, miserable, poor, blind and naked."* Herein, Christ warns that such a stage of seductive deception will lead to a state of spiritual blindness, apathy and indifference, where we are neither hot nor cold. Therefore, the writer says that Christ will spit, spew or vomit that person from His mouth and from His church. To experience such a state is the ultimate form of rejection from God, as they will utterly parish in their destruction.

Many passages, such as the one found in Timothy 6:3-10, warn us about the dangerous temptations and perilous traps that wait to ensnare those who desire to be rich. As false teachers go about planting and spreading seeds for "the love of money", then the fruit and crops produced from their messages are evil in nature, because the root is evil. For this reason some have strayed from the faith. If we want to uproot seeds of greed for money and counter act and counter balance the doctrine of wealth, we must return again to the gospel message of Jesus Christ, and Him crucified. And we must denounce the error of extremes like the doctrine of wealth, and recommit ourselves once again to the task and message of fighting the good fight of faith. That is the kind of sound doctrine that we must return to.

Weapons of War in Faith

Now that we have examined ourselves and found that we are truly in the faith, and made a conscious decision to engage our opponents by contending for the faith, then we must understand and choose what instruments and techniques we have at our disposal to effectively defend ourselves and our position in the faith. First and foremost, we must understand the nature of the weapons available to us. The Bible says that the weapons of our warfare are not carnal or earthly, but they are mighty through God, to the pulling down of strongholds. This passage reveals that the nature of our weaponry is two fold; it is both spiritual and intellectual in nature.

As soldiers of the cross, we are instructed to put on the whole armor of God (Ephesians 6:13-17). The armor at our disposal is comprised of both defensive and offensive elements. We are told to put on the girdle of truth and the breastplate of righteousness. Next, we are to shoe our feet with the gospel of peace and protect our head with the helmet of salvation. Please note that these are defensive elements of the armor. Above all, we are instructed to take the shield of faith. Why is faith so important? Consider the fact that a shield can be used as a defensive tool or an offensive weapon. It can be use to protect one's self from the arrows and blows of the enemy; or it can be use to overpower the enemy by striking and pressing against him. Faith is both defensive and offensive in its application; hence to learn to operate in faith is one of the most importance tools at our disposal.

Finally, we are told to take the sword of the spirit as an offensive instrument of warfare. We must understand that the primary weapon available to the believer is the Word of God. This is the greatest tool in our arsenal. The familiar in Hebrews 4:12 states, ***"For the word of God is living and powerful, and sharper than any two-edged sword, piercing even to the division of soul and spirit, and of joints and marrow, and is a discerner of the thoughts and intents of the heart."*** The Apostle Paul specifically says the Word is sharper than **any** two edge sword. This would have been a very powerful statement for the first-century Christians who received this information. They would have understood the writer's use of symbolism, and his comparison of the word of God, with a Roman two-edged sword. According to historians and researchers of Rome at Optimus International[17], "The Romans were masters at adopting and modifying sword designs to overcome disadvantages in combat. Improvements to Roman swords were often based upon technology from other cultures like the Greeks, Celts and Spanish. This allowed Romans to have a different sword for each warfare strategy."

The most recognizable and famous of all the designs was known as the Roman short sword. Soldiers employed up to five different visions of the Roman short sword. The most common was called the Pompeii Gladius, while the long sword of choice was called the double-edged Roman Spatha. First-century Christians would have certainly understood that it was by the use of this weapon, that Rome was able to conquer the entire known world of its day. This is the kind of power available to us through the word of God!

Now consider the fact that every Roman soldier had to be trained to develop the necessary skill and technique to wield his sword with the greatest ability. This means that we too must become skilled in our use of the Word of God. We must follow the instructions of

2Timothy 2:15, which admonishes us to, "Be diligent to present yourself approved to God, a worker who does not need to be ashamed, rightly dividing the word of truth." Our study of the word of God will help us to develop our skills in a technique and ability known as the **art of apologetics**.

✝
Chapter Eleven
CHARISMATIC APOLOGETICS

Definition of Christian Apologetics

One of the necessary communication skills we need to develop within the charismatic community is the use of something called apologetics. Apologetic skills allow an individual to effectively communicate what he or she believes in a clear, concise and systematic manner. Such beliefs are then supported by evidence such as, the truth of scripture, historical facts, science and other verifiable documented information, for the purpose of building a strong and credible case with correct conclusions and truths to support those beliefs.

The practice of apologetic debate has been around for thousands of years. During the time of Hebraic antiquity, Jewish scholars competed for influence and notoriety within the religious realm of Judaism. According to ancient Jewish tradition, such debates took place quite frequently between rival schools of thought. One notable teacher that had a great impact upon Jewish thinking was a scholar by the name of Hillel. His approach to interpreting Mosaic Law reportedly focused on the spirit of the Law. His style of teaching combined short memorable sayings with insightful interpretation.

The school or house of Hillel represented the very opposite approach to another influential school of thought known as the house of Shammai. Unlike Hillel, rabbi Shammai took a more unyielding legalistic approach to interpreting Mosaic Law. His application of the law was demonstrated through tedious, ritualistic efforts designed to reflect true piety and spirituality. Because of their differences of approach and opinions, the house of Shammai and the house of Hillel were continually at odds with each other. Therefore, debates were used as a forum to express the competing ideas of each school of ancient Judaism.

In the twentieth century, men like C.S. Lewis and Francis Schaeffer came to the forefront of Christian apologetics. Lewis and others from his day are regarded as excellent Christian thinkers and apologist who championed the cause Christianity in the postmodern era. They were able to confront the secular intellectual elite, who opposed the ideas and beliefs of the Christian faith, in a way that was both anointed and ingenious.

Although in the past, apologetics has generally dealt with issues such as the existence of God and creation vs. the theory of evolution, more recent developments have shifted the focus to issues that should be considered peripheral issues within Christendom. In house debating can be a opportunity for healthy discussion of Christian thoughts and ideas, but far too often in recent times, some Evangelical advocates of apologetics have turned the discussions into unhealthy and divisive arguments that produce strife and harmful injuries to Charismatic Christians, and other Christian communities as well.

Christians like those within Catholic, Evangelical Lutheran and Methodist camps, have become very effective at developing their apologetic skills and responses. It seems as if those individuals and ministries who practice apologetic skills intimidate many within the charismatic community. But we need not be intimidated. In fact, it is absolutely imperative that we learn to embrace and utilize the same skills, so that we too may be able to defend our position in the faith. Especially, in response to individuals within the body of Christ who vigorously oppose our position on controversial issues, within the faith. Such topics as healing, prosperity, miracles, signs and wonders, the operation of the spiritual gifts, and other charismatic issues are at the center of in-house Christian debates.

However, it has been an uneven debate, primarily because of our reluctance to show up for the argument, and a failure to effectively communicate and represent a biblical-charismatic position, regarding these subjects and other topics, specific to the charismatic viewpoint. Although such topics should be considered secondary issues, nevertheless, they represent characteristics of the charismatic community that make us valuable and unique, within the body of Christ. Therefore, it is important that we equip ourselves to defend what God has given to us, by way of His Holy Spirit, before further damage has been done to the faith of believers within the charismatic community.

As we begin our journey into the arena of apologetic debate, it is important for the charismatic Christian to understand several critical aspects of the argument that we must present. First and foremost, before we even attempt to get into the ring, we must be prepared to fight. The reason we must be prepared to fight is that our very life in the body of Christ is at stake. We are facing a detrimental onslaught, both in terms of our position in the body and the spiritual lives of charismatic believers in the faith, from three distinct and very different adversaries.

Trilateral Opposition in the Faith

First of all, we are under attack from the spiritual forces that oppose every born again believer, therefore we must always understand that our primary enemy is non other than the devil and his spiritual henchmen. We are reminded again from the word of God to, ***"Put on the whole armor of God, that you may be able to stand against the wiles of the devil. For we wrestle not against flesh and blood, but against principalities, against powers, against the rulers of the darkness of this age, against spiritual host of wickedness in heavenly places.*** (Ephesians 4:11,12)" At one time, this kind of revelation helped to define the charismatic Christian, but once again, it is this kind of truth that we have gotten away from in our pulpit and pews. We have exchanged the blessing of these spiritual treasures for the carnal pursuit of "blessings and bling." Therefore in preparation for the fight it is high time that we get back to our roots and ask the Lord to give us a fresh revelation and application of this truth.

Secondly, we must understand that the next source of opposition we face is not just the enemy without, but also our brother within. As I mentioned early on in chapter ten on *Faith under Fire*, there has been a vicious malicious onslaught from certain Evangelical apologetic leaders in other Christian camps. Whether their efforts are intentional or not, the affects are the same, in that a great many charismatic Christians have been detrimentally wounded by their deliberate attacks upon character and position of the charismatic community of faith. It is for this reason that we must equip ourselves to defend our position in the faith and to bring comfort, confidence and restoration to the many believers that have been affected by anti-charismatic teachings.

The third threat and possible the most dangerous opposition we face is corruption from within, because of false teachers and apostate preachers within our community. Much of the attention and negative commentary directed toward the Word of Faith community is due to the erroneous and misguided teaching that has become so prevalent within our ranks. Therefore we must arm ourselves to resist and counter the detrimental affects of their unbalanced and unbiblical teachings by developing a solid apologetic foundation that brings us back to the word of God, in the true Word of Faith tradition.

Just as scripture teaches us that as individual believers, we face opposing forces from three sources, the world the flesh and the devil, the same principle and model is at work on a corporate level within the body of Christ. Together, these three sources of opposition represent the greatest threat to the charismatic position in the faith.

And together, they pose the greatest danger to the survival and well being of charismatic Christians everywhere. It is for these reasons that we have the responsibility to develop a strong apologetic response in defense of the charismatic position in the faith and body of our Lord and Savior Jesus Christ.

Building Confidence in the Faith

One of the more positive reasons to develop a solid apologetic response in defense of the charismatic position is to build the overall confidence of believers within the community of faith. Not only does this include believers within the charismatic community, but also those Christians and seekers who have direct contact with the community on every level. In fact this could prove to be one of the best assets and greatest benefits of entering the charismatic Christian debate. But first, let's take a look at the things I believe we have gotten right concerning this one-sided debate.

In recent years, there has been an increased awareness about the concerns and criticisms that others within the body of Christ have expressed against us. Although it was almost impossible to ignore, it is a very good thing that we have finally realized that there is a debate going on, at which we seem to be at the very center. Just the realization of this fact can begin to provide a basis for building our confidence because it speaks to the powerful voice and influential ability of the Charismatic Movement within the body of Christ. Therefore we can be assured of our position because, God has already provided a platform in faith and grace, from which we may speak the truth in love concerning His purpose and plan for the Word of Faith message. And now that we have come to this realization, it is time to affirm our presence and position within the body of Christ, using a clear, intentional apologetic method.

Another area, where I believe we got it right, was our refusal to engage in unbiblical argumentative behavior. This is one action, or reaction that may be the most commendable. For the most part, it has been the position of the charismatic community and its leadership not to respond in kind, to the confrontational and divisive rhetoric conducted by many who represent the Evangelical apologetic community.

One passage of scripture that proponents of Christian apologetics use to support their engagement in offensive apologetic practices is found in 2Timothy 2:15. But closer examination of this passage, in light of its overall context, reveals that the authority of scripture condemns such aggressive confrontational behavior. In the passage, it is the fourteenth verse that clearly establishes the context for verse fifteen, as well as the remainder of the chapter. In verse fourteen, Paul encourages Timothy, *"not to strive about words to no profit, to the ruin of the hearers."* Paul's instruction to Timothy continues in verse twenty-three, which tells us to *"avoid foolish an ignorant disputes; knowing that they generate strife..."*

Therefore, refusal of most charismatic Christians to engage the debate and their tendency to shun the possibility of disputes and arguments that generate strife have proved to be an act of obedience to the instruction and authority of scripture. In this action, we can take comfort and have confidence in the God who honors obedience above sacrifice. It is He who is on our side! Amen. However, I also believe that failure to engage the debate is due, at least in part, to the following reasons:

- Failure and reluctance to engage is due to ignorance and uncertainty about the specific role and value that God has assigned to the charismatic community as a member of the body.
- Clarity and definition has been lost due to a drift away from the foundational teachings that were taught during the early days of the charismatic movement.
- General ignorance and lack of education about scriptural, historical and factual evidence, which

supports a credible defense for the charismatic position.

- Failure to respond and engage may be due in part to an attempt to walk in love by ignoring the attacks of critics and the anti-charismatic commentary they promote.

Although we have been reluctant and unwilling in the past to engage the critics because of one or more of these reasons, it is time to begin to build our level of confidence in the faith and in our community. Truth be told, we have just as much credible evidence to support the charismatic position of faith and revelation, as does any other evangelical Christian apologetic. When we become familiar with the history of the Christian faith and skilled with an understanding of the rules of apologetic debate, we will then gain the confidence we need to engage the opposition, with evidence that weighs heavily in our favor.

Cogitating Charismatic Christians

Well, some may ask, "Where do I start and how do I begin?" The answer is as simple as eating pie. It is all about what you eat. As charismatic Christians, we are used to eating everything that has to do with *faith*, but the time has come to expand our diet to include information for **intellectual reason.** Let's face it! The average charismatic believer may know who Charles Capps is, but may have no clue of who Charles Spurgeon was. They can easily quote Kenneth Hagin, but have great difficulty quoting anything from C.S. Lewis or Francis Schaeffer. Therefore, it starts by simply familiarizing ourselves with a few of the great apologetic thinkers of our time. In turn, we will be better equipped to deal with the anti-charismatic apologist, because we will have become more familiar with the informational sources that they use to try to discredit charismatic Christian theology.

The good news is things are beginning to change and the tide has begun to turn. I recently had the opportunity to attend an apologetic debate which proves this point. Although I have attended a few forums of this kind, truth be told, I have never experienced a Christian apologetic debate quite like this one. The very first notable difference about this particular debate was the fact that it was hosted by a charismatic church! The second notable difference was the fact that it was sponsored and attended by a local African American charismatic congregation. In my experience, such forums are usually held at more traditional, Caucasian, denominational churches or college campuses, with mostly Eurocentric Christian representation. But this one was different. This was huge! And maybe even historic, at lest for this Midwest community. So I decided to ask the pastor of the church for an interview. We agreed to meet at his church for an interview that lasted about an hour.

He is Reverend Willie R. McMiller Sr., pastor of Brotherly Love West Christian Assembly church in Jennings, Missouri. As we began our conversation, I asked Pastor McMiller to tell me a little bit about him and how he came to Christ. With a nod of his head and a winning smile, he said that he was born and raised in Blytheville, Arkansas, just below the Missouri boot heel. At the age of nineteen, he moved from the small town of Blytheville to make a new life for himself in the big city of Los Angeles, California. He briefly spoke about his journey to find the truth and how he investigated the claims of some other religions. But after about four years of living life in the big city, Pastor McMiller says "The Lord brought me out of a bad situation." After which he moved back to Arkansas, where the Lord saved him in 1978 and began to prepare him for ministry.

I then told him how much I enjoyed the formal debate I attended at his church and asked what the catalyst for his interest in apologetics was. Pastor McMiller responded by saying, "Well when the Lord saved me, he put me in the church I was born and raised in. And there was a deacon there, and I remember everywhere he went, he had his Bible and his Wycliffe commentary. Those were his two books. And when we were up there teaching Sunday school, he would have his little commentary. I said, 'I'm going to get me one of those,' you see, because he would always bring in another element of truth to try to help us exegete the scriptures. So that was my first taste of really getting into the extra biblical stuff when it comes to study. He then talked me into getting a good study bible, a Scholfield Bible. Then from there I just started to stock up on a lot of commentary from people like Albert Barns and W. E. Vines, so I got me a little Greek dictionary. I just stocked up on other commentaries to look at other perspectives. Not so much buying into all of them, but at least studying them to see what others had to say."

Next, I wanted to know what prompted him to host such an event at his church. Without hesitation, Pastor McMiller responded, "I came out of the Church of God in Christ and my mother and grandmother were members, so that was really all I knew. And it was a great church for indoctrinating into "here's what we do" and "here's what we believe." But how to defend that (indoctrination) from a scriptural point of view and in an apologetic way; they didn't prepare us for that. So the Lord put it in my heart and said, "When you start to pastor, teach the people!"

The Lord put it in my spirit to equip the saints to defend the gospel. To defend what we believe. As the writer of the Bible tells us, "Be ready to give an answer to any man that asks you any question about the hope that lies within you." The Lord said to upgrade the IQ of the saints." And that's what we're trying to do; we're trying to upgrade the IQ of the saints. Then there are those who come to me and say, "Well I was hit with this on the job," or "My family member is a Jehovah's Witness," or whatever and ask, "How do I deal with that?" So that was the genesis of the small group studies where we have a topic for study and discussion. And for some, we actually use a debate format, as when you were here the other night." I was excited and ever so grateful to see that believers within the charismatic community have begun to embrace the use of apologetic skills to support their Christian faith.

Pastor McMiller then said something that rang with such truth in my spirit. He continued by saying, "When we decided to hold a formal debate, I didn't want to bring another group in from that camp because so often, and I've been involved in those, where it's not really a debate, it's an argument." Before I knew it, I was shouting, "That's right! That is so right! ...," in affirmation of what he had just said. He quickly followed my exclamation by saying, "I was involved in one just a couple of weeks ago, where it was rigid, it was accusatory, it was trying to show others where you're just wrong; instead of using a debate format in a manner where we can do this in a civil way. So I wanted to stay away from those kinds of elements in our debates."

Finally regarding this topic, I asked Pastor Willie R. McMiller about what, if any, had been the greatest challenges he has faced in attempting to teach charismatic Christians to become more intellectual in there approach to the study of the scriptures. He said, "We want people that are rooted and grounded in the truth. It's a challenge as a pastor because we are good "at having church." And so I'll here someone say, 'That was a good message,' or they might say 'Oh, we had church today!' And I'll ask, 'Well what was the message,' or 'What was the text?' In a moment of amusement and laughter, we both stated the obvious, saying "They can't tell you!" He continued, "And I do believe that we are supposed to worship God in spirit and in truth, but so often as (charismatic) Christians, we get caught up in the spiritual and emotional side (of worship) that we neglect the truth. I tell the people that we sing about a Jesus that we really don't know. We shout over things that we really don't know what we are shouting about. So let's get some word in us. Let's get educated in the word. Then we will understand why we do what we do."

At this point in the conversation, Pastor McMiller wanted to make his intentions clear, as he affirmed his charismatic position.

He said, "Please understand, I'm not trying to take us into another denomination. I believe in my charismatic roots. I believe in the charismatic gifts. And we preach, teach and operate in those gifts. But I do think that there is room for scriptural knowledge and being able to exegete scripture; to get into the word and be able to defend it apologetically." Pastor McMiller then made a very insightful observation that appropriately describes the process. He said, "Speaking of bringing the people to this point, really what we are doing is changing people's diet. And that's not always easy!" Needless to say, I was absolutely elated because that is exactly what the Lord said to me, when he began to talk to me about the importance of this issue.

As he continued to elaborate by saying, "Even though, in this health conscious society in which we live, we know that eating certain food is not good for us, but that's what we're used to. So now when I put something healthy in front of you, it's not as palatable, it's not as satisfying; even though it's better for you. So we're trying to bring people from an exclusively emotional based worship and celebration to where we are now going to study. We want to break this thing down. We've got to dig, because the bible lets us know that the Spirit of God searches the deep things of God. Search meaning to excavate, so we got to go deep, we've got to do some excavation here. And that kind of worship sticks with you better than just some emotional high that you had. Where you can't talk about how you got there, but all you know is that you got there. So changing our diet is a difficult thing, in that we are telling the people, "Ok. We will shout in a few minute, but right now let's get into the Word."

As we continued our discussion about the challenges and difficulties associated with equipping the charismatic community with apologetic skills, we both agreed that the goal the message, and indeed of this book, is to bring people to a position of balance. One of the primary characteristics and objectives of the early Word of Faith movement was to build strong and balanced Christians. Since balance is really the key to living a successful Christian life, we must be willing to move toward a position of balance that creates what some might call a hybrid model of Christianity. Such a hybrid is formed when the cogitating (intellectual or thinking) Christian seeks to become more charismatic and charismatic Christians become more intellectual in their Christianity. Although this may sound like a new idea to some folk, I believe this is the model of Christianity that Jesus and Paul presented to the body of Christ, from the very beginning of the Church.

As charismatic Christians, we must realize that God never required us to hang up our thinking caps to become a spiritual giant.

191

By the same token, Evangelical believers should also understand that it is possible to be both an intellectual and charismatically gifted believer. It is like two sides of the same coin; to present one without the other is to only acknowledge one side and not the other. To present such a coin or bill as legal tender is to present counterfeit currency and to engage in illegal activity. In like manner, this is what so many Christians do when it comes to the issue of intellectual reason verses charismatic spiritual gifts. Evangelicals try to represent Christianity without acknowledging and embracing the need for charismatic supernatural attributes. By the same token (no pun intended), charismatic Christians wish to focus on the supernatural and emotional aspects of Christianity, without building their cognitive ability and engaging in the intellectual arenas of the Christian faith. To represent the true model of Christian ministry, we must be willing to embrace both sides of the proverbial coin.

This presents a wonderful opportunity for the Charismatic believer to really demonstrate the kind of Pauline type ministry that has been missing from the landscape of the Church for a long time. As we demonstrate the ability to meet both the spiritual needs of people, and to address the intellectual arguments of our day, we are modeling the kind of ministry that Jesus Himself displayed. This is the kind of power and understanding that he gave to His disciples as He sent them out and said, *"Go therefore and make disciples of all nations…Heal the sick, cleanse the lepers, raise the dead, cast out devils. Freely you have received, freely give."* (Matthew 28:19, 10:8)

✝ Chapter Twelve

CHARISMATIC CULTS

Some may ask the questions, "What is a charismatic cult, what does it look like, and what do they believe?" To answer these questions we should consider the biblical and historical model that we find throughout the history of the Church. From the very beginning of Church history, there have been groups that claimed to be Christian and appeared to be Christ-like, but in reality were not followers of Christ.

One of the best examples of such a group would be a sect of the first-century Church who became known as the Gnostic believers. This ancient community of faith was sect of early Christianity that believed Jesus had some "secret knowledge" that He wanted to impart to His believers. As they sought to be enlightened, they encouraged others to become enlightened as well, through their claim of divine secret knowledge. This flawed and misguided pursuit for some mystical revelation and magical manifestations led to deception and error.

Although it appears from the historical record that the Gnostics were very involved in the affairs of the early Church, but their participation was limited because of their error. Efforts to influence the Church through doctrine and even their suggestions for the canonization of the scriptures were met with rejection. Eventually, the Gnostics were deemed to be too far beyond the pale of orthodoxy to be considered a Christian sect. By the turn of the third-century, they were declared heretical and apostate.

Well, not much has changed over the last two thousand years. In fact there may be even more religious groups who claim to have received some kind of secret knowledge from one god or another. As we begin to draw some correlation between this historical example and some modern day groups, we must remember to consider the inerrancy of scripture as the final authority for truth. Therefore we must be careful of ministries that try to encourage us to follow them because of some new and mysterious revelation of truth. And to make matters worse, factors such as "charismatic lingo" and the desire to be spiritually knowledgeable and "deep", simply increase the possibility for error within the Word of Faith community.

Therefore, claims of any new words of wisdom or revelation knowledge must not exceed the authority of scripture. Nor should the teaching of any preacher or teacher be exalted above the authority of scripture. In either case, any teaching that is found to be inconsistent with the canon of scripture should be rejected as truth and shunned as error. According to scripture, we should deal with such groups and individuals in love, but compel them to return to a biblical foundation for truth.

Next, we must define and reveal the difference between truth and error as it pertains to charismatic pedagogy. To continue with our modern day correlation, let's consider and compare some of the teachings that are prevalent within charismatic circles of the Church today. For example, many teachers in our community emphasize that we have been created in the image of God. This doctrine is true, but there are those who have begun to teach that since God created us in His image, then He has created us as "little gods."

While it is true that Jesus mentioned this fact in a conversation with the Pharisees, we must be careful when building entire doctrines from such statements. We must keep in mind that in the passage, Jesus is quoting the scripture as a rebuttal, in response to the Pharisees' question of His deity. He was using their knowledge of scripture as a point of reference to support His claim to deity, not ours. With just a little research, we find that the term "gods" refers to "mighty ones or judges." And as sons of GOD, we too have been given the Spirit of Might, the Holy Spirit, through whom, the saints will one day judge the world. Therefore, Jesus never said that His disciples were little gods. He called us servants, sons, friends, ambassadors, kings, priest and judges, but never deity as gods. This is however, the kind of error that occurs when we fail to apply a proper exegesis by violating basic laws of Hermeneutics. Such doctrines are erroneous and should be differentiated from the truth.

Statements like this are comparable to many New Age teachings. Therefore, such erroneous doctrines should be rejected and denounced by leaders of the true charismatic Christian church. After which, we must distance ourselves from those teachers and groups that continue to preach and teach doctrines that should be defined as heretical apostasy. Communities of faith that fail to remain consistent with the teachings of Christ and the orthodoxy of scripture can no longer be defined as Christian. Therefore, by definition of default, they become something other than Christian.

Making the Difference of Distinction

While on the subject of error in the Church, it is necessary to address the issue of apostasy, particularly as it relates to the charismatic community. The Bible clearly warns us about the apostate condition of believers in the last days. Therefore, it is of the utmost importance that we receive wise counsel from the word regarding this matter. In 2 Corinthians 11:3, the Apostle Paul expresses his concern for the Corinthian church because their willingness to tolerate false teachers while they questioned the validity of his apostolic authority. He begins in verse three, "3 *But I fear, let somehow, as the serpent deceived Eve by his craftiness, so your minds may be corrupted from the simplicity that is in Christ. 4 For if he who comes preaches another Jesus whom we have not preached, or if you receive a different spirit which you have not received, or a different gospel which you have not accepted – you may well put up with it!*"

Paul's concern for the Corinthian church is echoed in the Charismatic Church of today. In fact, the church at Corinth was the charismatic church of Paul's day. And despite confirmation of the truth of God's word, through the signs and wonders of the charisma gifts, they were still prone to fall for the seduction of sin and error. This is particularly crucial for the Word of Faith community because of a greater opportunity for error, due to the prominent operation of the gifts of the spirit in nondenominational churches. My concern, like Paul, is that we have way too much tolerance for messengers of error and agents of apostasy.

Let's face it! There is always someone in our community who is trying to share some kind of new revelation that they have supposedly received from God. Therefore, it behooves us to be ever so vigilant to maintaining a theological environment that is conducive to sound doctrine, while simultaneously remaining sensitive and open to true revelation from God. As a community of faith, this is the good fight of faith that we must engage in. It is necessary then to make a clear distinction between the Charismatic Church and groups that should be considered as charismatic cults. This delineation must be based upon criteria from the word of God, and not upon what we may think or feel. That criterion has been clearly set forth by the authority of scripture and there can be no deviation what so ever.

The Bible says if anyone, even an angel (messenger) from heaven comes preaching another Jesus, or another gospel, let that person be accursed. (Galatians 1:8, 9) And if anyone denies that Jesus is the Christ or that He has not come in the flesh, then that person is not of God. Therefore, we are instructed to test the spirit of the messenger by the Spirit of God. (1 John 4:1-3) These are just a few of the scriptural references we must use when determining the standard for sound doctrine. We have a clear mandate from scripture to equip ourselves for the purpose of recognizing false teaching and for the defense of the gospel of Jesus Christ.

Because so many have forsaken their faith in Christ and exchanged the truth for a lie, it is necessary that we begin to identify those who have crept into our midst, and begin to distance ourselves from their deceptive doctrines. By God's grace, we can limit the detrimental influence of false teachers within the charismatic community who contribute to the dysfunction and disaffiliation of many from our ranks, and the apostasy of others from the faith.

Unity in the Fight

This is where we would do well to enlist the counsel and aid of our brethren in the Evangelical community. They have become skilled in the area of apologetics. Such a collaboration of faith would prove to be advantageous for the charismatic and evangelical members alike. One obvious reason is that we could benefit from the knowledge and wisdom they have gained as defenders of the faith. Secondly, it would create an opportunity for dialogue between both sides of the charismatic debate. But even more importantly, it would allow each side to deal with areas of error and sin in their respective camp.

The challenge for many leaders within the charismatic community would be to repent of the sin of pride and arrogance. The word tells us "knowledge puffs up." Therefore, the source of pride for many charismatic preachers and teachers stems from the fact that we are extremely well versed in the scriptures; and from the amount of revelation knowledge we have received. This is the sin that is so apparent among prominent preachers and teachers. In fact it is so visible that they almost seem to wear their pride, like a suit, for every message they preach. Some even seem to act as if they have achieved superstar status. We must repent of such arrogance and sin. A request for dialogue would present the opportunity for repentance and submission before God and our evangelical brethren. Such an act would reflect an outward expression of true Christianity, love and humility.

A request for dialogue could prove to be just as much a challenge for our evangelical counterparts as well. Many of their apologetic representatives would also have to repent of the same sin of pride and arrogance. Because of pride from their knowledge of the Word, their ability to dominate the table of debate, they seem to project an arrogant, intellectually elite attitude toward other members of the body of Christ. They also appear to have the tendency to elevate the law of God above the love of God. Therefore, pride seems to prevent many apologetic teacher and preachers from walking in the greatest commandment, which is love. Again, such a tendency represents a sin of omission and error. To engage in a loving opportunity for dialogue would require repentance and submission to the law of love, and would reflect a genuine desire for communication and unity.

This should be the ultimate goal for both the evangelical and charismatic community. To agree to engage in an occasion for dialogue would present an opportunity to demonstrate the will of God, as it is presented in Paul's instruction to *"...walk worthy of the call to which you were called, with all lowliness, ...bearing with one another in love, endeavor to keep the unity of the Spirit, in the bond of peace."* (Ephesians 4:1-3) To this end, the Apostle Paul pleads with us to all speak the same thing, and that there would be no division among brethren in the body of Christ. (1 Corinthians 1: 10)

It is high time that we put away our petty differences and begin to exhibit the kind of unity that Paul has challenged us to display. Such a union would certainly show the world that the word of God is true when it says, "And all men will know that you are my disciples by your love for one another." Many of our apologetic evangelical brethren may say that the opportunity for debate has always been open. But please note that I did not use the term debate. To debate suggests a negative implication of an exercise in argumentative expression.

The term debate does not carry the same focus on communication as the word dialogue. Therefore, our goal is to come to the table of discussion to engage the debate in the attempt to create a positive dialogue. The end result should be repentance and communication based upon an expression of love, gentleness and humility.

Chapter Thirteen
REPENTANCE and RESTORATION

During my interview with Pastor Femi, one of the key issues we talked about was the absence of the balance once found within the teachings of popular charismatic ministries. As we talked about the problem of unbalanced teaching within our circles, he began to try to put it into context for us as believers. He said, "God is sovereign, right? Therefore, we are part of a bigger picture and I wish people would understand that. Our lives are relevant to God, but they are relevant to the bigger picture. So your blessings, or the lack of it, are part of a bigger tapestry. And when you submit and yield to the Holy Spirit, then it doesn't really matter what He does.

And faith is the substance of things hoped for and the evidence of things that are not seen. Now there is no hope when it is in your hand, right? And it is not "unseen" when it is right in front of you. So what we are trying to do many times is to circumvent and undermine the process of faith. You know…we don't want to wait; we want to see it-show me! But it is not necessarily about showing you, it is about believing; even when you have not seen. You know, "Blessed are they who believe and have not seen." But it's becoming a thing where people say, "Well if I see it then I'll believe."

He continued by saying, "The Word of Faith movement by itself is error; 'by itself.' But in combination with everything else; in combination with holiness, in combination with contentment, and in combination of service and love, then yes that is fine. There is a scripture in the Bible that I like. It says that we do not receive because we do no ask. And when we ask, we ask amiss, because we ask to squander on ourselves. Now the Word of Faith focuses on yourselves; how you can use the word of God to get what you want. But Jesus Christ came and He worked for other people. So there is a giving of one's self for others.

We like to talk about Philippians 4:19, *"For my God shall supply all of your needs according to His riches and glory,"* but let's go back up and look at 4:15. It talks about your ministry to the saints, in that you are ministering to the saints, God is not unrighteous to forget your labor of love. So there is a balance to it! You can't walk around casting mountains into the ocean just so that you can build another big house. But if in the course of serving God, loving your neighbor, doing His will and the mountain stood in your way; then you can say as the Bible says. The Bible says, "Who art thou oh mountain before Zerubbabel? You shall be made as a pebble." But Zerubbabel was doing the work of God; he was doing the will of God. And when the mountain stood in the way he could speak to the mountain. But if in the course of squandering on your own lust, the mountain stands in your way, you can speak to the mountain until you are blue in the face (and nothing will happen) because you are not relevant to the purpose of God.

And that is a problem with the Word of Faith movement! It doesn't teach people to be relevant to God. They are relevant to themselves. You know, it's just…people read the Bible so that they can find tools on how to get rich. There is a proverb in Nigeria where I come from that says, "There are many roads to the market," and Christianity has become just another road to the market. And what is the market? Wealth, power, and fame! And if Christianity becomes like the world, if we have the same goals as everybody else, then we are no better than the world. Well the Bible says that we are in the world, but we are not of the world and we should not be like the world, because the things of the world are enmity with God. But Christianity has become another road to get to fame, wealth and power."

After Pastor Femi's insightful response, I asked if he thought that this was a point of error that had taken place in the Word of Faith/ Charismatic movement. As he considered my question he responded by saying, "I won't call it error, I call it imbalance." I chuckled with joyful corroboration as I affirmed his description and diagnosis of the problem. He too continued in affirmation and reiterated, "Yes I call it imbalance. I call it some folks taking part of the Bible and scripture, and putting so much weight on it that they tip the scales. You know... and then you have a problem."

Balance is the Key

In the book of Revelation, Jesus told the Angel of the church at Ephesus to write saying, *"I know your works, and your labor, your patience, and that you cannot bear those who are evil. Nevertheless, I have this against you, that you have left your first love."* (Revelation 2:1) You see, in the beginning it wasn't the love of money or wealth that characterized the movement. It was simply our love for Jesus and that, "Dare to believe God for anything!" kind of faith that set us apart and defined us as a movement. Although we have made many contributions to the body of Christ, built mega-churches and done lots of other good things, these are not the things for which we should be known. Instead, we ought to be remembered for our contributions of love and faithfulness to GOD, for our obedience to His word and to His heavenly vision, and for our love for one another.

To remain a contributing member of the body of Christ, we must return to our first love, just as the Apostle John wrote to the church of Ephesus in the book of Revelation. He writes, *"Remember therefore from where you have fallen; repent and do the first works, or else I will come to you quickly and remove your lampstand from its place, unless you repent."* (Revelation 2:5) This means returning to a more balanced approach in our preaching and teaching of the Word. Therefore we should continue to preach and teach the message of divine health and wellness as it pertains to healing is for the Christian today, while placing the greater emphasis on the message of healing through the forgiveness of sin, which God provides to ultimately minister to the sin sick condition of mankind apart from Christ.

This has been the ministry and message of the Charismatic Church from the very beginning. It has been a message of balance, truth and love. It has been a ministry that calls the Church back to the truth of scripture, with a desire to bring healing, prosperity and freedom to believers of every denominational affiliation. That's the kind of ministry and message we must return to. Please understand that I am not suggesting that we abandon the truths from scripture and the divinely inspired revelations that have been given to us by God, which make us specifically unique and valuable to the body of Christ. But I do say there is no way we can abandon the essential doctrines of the Christian Church and still expect to remain a viable and important tool in God's end-time army and arsenal of faith.

Restoration and Deliverance

Now is the time when pastors of local nondenominational churches and charismatic Christian centers must lead their congregations in repentance, re-education and affirmation of the basic tenants of the Christian faith. We must begin again to emphasize the redemptive work of Christ, His salvation through the Cross of Calvary, and the promise of resurrection hope and life everlasting through Jesus Christ our Lord. We must again emphasize the need for Christians to live a holy and godly life, while continuing to proclaim the freedom and abundance offered by God, to those who choose to live a balanced life of faith and obedience.

Far too often it seems that the proponents of either side appear to ignore and undermine the necessity of both facets of this truth. It's like two sides of the same coin or dollar bill. Both sides must be stamped or printed and are necessary to be accepted as legal tender. And any coin or dollar bill that has been minted or printed baring only one side is rejected by the U.S. Department of Treasury and deemed unfit to represent legal currency. Any coin or bill with only one side that is represented as legitimate currency is considered a counterfeit representation.

So it is in the body of Christ! For leaders who represent the ranks of Reform theology to assert that the charismatic grace to operate in the gifts of the Spirit is in some way counterfeit, while emphasizing the importance of intellectual apologetic prowess, is unbalanced and erroneous. Or to condemn the prosperity message as error, while teaching that 'money is the root of all evil' and 'poverty is godly', is just as erroneous as what you seek to condemn. Therefore, balance is the key to representing an accurate representation of the biblical model for charismatic Christianity. It is through this balanced biblical approach that charismatic believers can earn the respect and appreciation that is fitting of the ministry to which we have been called.

Formula for Repentance and Restoration

In the charismatic community we like simple and easy formulas for success in Christ. Remember, God has promised, *"If My people who are called by My name will humble themselves, and pray and seek My face, and turn from their wicked ways, then I will hear from heaven, and will forgive their sin and heal their land"* (2Chronicles 7:14). This is the biblical formula for success in Christ. First of all, we are instructed to humble ourselves. Since the Bible says *"Pride come before destruction and a haughty spirit before a fall,"* then we can reasonably conclude that the destruction and the fall that follows pride and a haughty spirit can both be avoided. God has promised that He will provide the necessary strength and means to do so. James 4:6 emphasizes the fact that *"God resist the proud, but gives more grace to the humble."* It is through His impartation of grace that we are able to discern and divest ourselves of ungodly pride. Such pride emanates from Satan him self, however, the grace of God empowers us with the ability to resist his efforts to tempt us with fleshly inclinations of arrogance. Thus the scripture reads, *"Therefore, submit to God. Resist the devil and he will flee from you. (James 4:7)"* True humility is expressed in our willingness to submit to God. Humility is the first key to success. Therefore, our first key for successful repentance and restoration is to divest ourselves of all pride and haughtiness.

Secondly, the passage then says that we are to pray. This of course denote coming to God for the purpose of confession and communication. We are to petition and entreat the Lord according to His will and His word. However, such petitions and request must demonstrate an earnest effort and desire from the heart, to find out the will of God and what He has to say. Therefore, we must seek His face, which denotes pressing past our feelings, situation, circumstances and spiritual opposition, to find and enter in to His presence. That is where we will receive that rhema word we need that will grant us deliverance that comes from the final step. So then, earnest prayer and confession coupled with an effort to press beyond ourselves and into the presence of God is the second key to successful repentance and restoration.

Finally, the passage says if His people will, "*...turn from their wicked ways.*" And what are our wicked ways? Again, consider the fact that too many of our prominent charismatic preachers and teachers continue to communicate an unbalanced, one-sided description of the Prosperity Message. They have gone the way of the world as they reflect the image and values of Hollywood. They promote a counterfeit version of the Word of Faith message and misrepresent the charismatic Christian community. And as a community of faith, we have become double minded in our approach to Christianity. In effect, the charismatic movement has become adulterous in our pursuit of fortune, fame and freedom. To our shame, the scripture says, *"Adulterers and adulteresses! Do you not know that friendship* *with the world is enmity with God? Whoever therefore wants to be a friend of the world makes himself an enemy of God.* (James 4:4)"

Therefore, the third and final step in the process is repentance in the true sense of the word. James 4:8 instructs us to *"Draw near to God and He will draw near to you. Cleanse your hands, you sinners; and purify your hearts, you double minded."* We can not simply say what God says, then do something all together different and continue to go our own way. First we must stop; which means we must resolve within in our self to cease from our own works. In our heart and mind, we refuse to proceed any further, and that decision is reflected through our actions. Next we are to intentionally change course by turning away from the direction of sin and disobedience. Last but not least, we turn to the Word of God and proceed in the direction that leads to good instruction and godly behavior. Turning away from our will to pursue His will is the third and final key to successful repentance and restoration. The result of this formula for repentance and restoration is three fold; *"I will hear from heaven, and I will forgive their sin, and heal their land."*

Chapter Fourteen
FAITH FOR THE END TIME

Toward the end of every interview granted by each of my esteemed colleagues in the gospel and friends in the faith, I took the opportunity to ask some questions that I believe, should be at the forefront of the charismatic Christian experience today. I asked each of the individuals I had the pleasure to interview, what kind of changes did they expect to see in the direction and ministry of the Charismatic Movement? Can we get back on track and expect a return to the kind of miraculous manifestations of God's glory, as in the early days of the movement? Can we move forward and will it be a change for the better?

Or are we destined to remain in a powerless state of flux and doomed to fall into the same impotent state of faith, which plagues so many of our fellow communities within the body of Christ. What changes might be looming just over the horizon that may affect the Word of Faith community and its mission to fulfill the Great Commission? These were certainly among the first questions I wanted to ask, but thought it best to save the best for last.

Changing Winds of Charismatic Trends

In keeping with the purpose of this book, I wanted to talk with pastors and lay leaders involved in the ministry, about changes and trends that they have noticed in the charismatic community and the Church at large. Minister Virginia Martin was among the first to be ask what her thoughts were, concerning the fate and future of the Charismatic Movement. I asked if she felt the movement could be enhanced or better directed, and if so, how? She said that she recently had a conversation about this very issue with a friend the other day, because they missed the time when there really was, "a move of God" in the service. To my surprise, she responded without hesitation. "I don't think as it was, it can be anymore. Because I think that it has evolved into something different!" As she thoughtfully constructed her answer, she continued by saying, "I think that people are taking what they got from there [the Charismatic/Word-Faith community], and then they are taking what they had from their background, and then they are meshing those into something altogether different."

I asked her to elaborate on what she meant by "something altogether different." And how did she believe it was taking place? She continued to explain by saying, "It's the teaching from there [the Charismatic/Word-Faith community], but it's the flavor from their background." She concluded by saying that people are taking certain aspects of the charismatic worship experience (i.e. the contemporary flavor, the freedom and the praise/worship music), and integrating it into their traditional worship experience, to form an entirely new experience in worship.

Minister Virginia's astute observation accurately describes one of the major trends taking place within the body of Christ. It certainly explains "the new flavor" of more than a few churches I have attended in recent times. The best way I can describe some of those local churches is to say that they are a blend of charismatic attributes with traditional denominational institutions. A case in point, would be the Charismatic-Baptist fellowship, I attended while visiting my wife's cousin in Kansas City, Missouri. It was a wonderful worship experience, complete with familiar worship and praise music and Bible verses that accompanied the sermon, all presented on a dual media screen display. However, the spirit and style of the service was distinctly Baptist in both the style of preaching, and the selections and sound of the choir.

Another example would be a charismatic Methodist church we attended, while on a trip to Pensacola, Florida a couple of years ago. That church was different because the overall feel of the service was very traditional, but the minister's message and style of "teaching" and preaching was refreshingly contemporary and charismatic. The affects of this trend can clearly be seen in various ways throughout the entire spectrum of Christianity. Such changes can be directly attributed to the impact and influence of the charismatic church upon more traditional, denominational communities.

In my own local church, for example, we have experienced a classic case of what has been called, "the worship wars." The conflict began about five years ago, when the pastor wanted to introduce a new and more contemporary worship style and format to our traditional Lutheran congregation. Needless to say, a real uphill battle ensued, as many of the traditional Lutheran members, who were resistant to changes of any kind, opposed the introduction and inclusion of contemporary worship and praise music. However, after much prayerful intercession and pastoral reassurance, the church recently made the decision to include a "Living Praise" format for those who desire a contemporary worship alternative, while continuing to offer the traditional worship style that other members were accustomed to.

In addition to this, the decision to incorporate contemporary worship format, facilitated the use of another tool that is indicative of the charismatic worship experience. On the first Sunday of the introduction of the new worship style, there in plain sight, was an extremely attractive, wood-framed media screen, mounted aptly above the congregation. This wonderful surprise hung there, like a symbol of acceptance and unification. As if to say, that the church had officially made the successful transition to contemporary worship and praise. To say the least, this was a major change for such a traditional Lutheran church. Nevertheless, the church leadership believes it is a step in the right direction, in an effort to meet the demands of a changing community in changing times.

I believe that this scenario is a vivid illustration of exactly what God is doing across the country and around the world. Christian communities are searching for ways to meet the responsibility to fulfill the Great Commission. As a result, a growing number of traditional churches are considering and implementing more charismatic approaches to ministry and worship. Again, I'm not asking you to simply take my word for it, so let's consider the facts.

Ever-Increasing Charismatic Faith

The Barna Research Group recently conducted a study, which included two new surveys that "indicate that things are changing dramatically in the religious landscape." According to Barna, "Those surveys – one among a national sample of adults and the other among a national sample of Protestant pastors – show that the number of churches and adherents to Pentecostal (or charismatic) perspectives and practices has grown significantly in the past two decades." According to the report[18] published by the Barna Group (founded by noted Christian sociologist George Barna), there has been a significant increase in the number of people who consider their selves to be a charismatic Christian.

The report cites the fact that "A decade ago, three out of ten adults claimed to be charismatic or Pentecostal Christians. Today, 36% of Americans accept that designation. That corresponds to approximately 80 million adults." The report noted, "(For the Barna survey, this included people who said they were a charismatic or Pentecostal Christian, that they had been "filled with the Holy Spirit" and who said they believe that "the charismatic gifts, such as tongues and healing, are still valid and active today.")

If this is true, these findings not only include new converts to the faith, but also include Evangelical members of traditional churches, who are beginning to accept and "redefine" themselves as charismatic evangelical Christians! The report said, "Charismatics are found throughout the fabric of American Christianity. Although just 8% of the population is evangelical, half of evangelical adults (49%) fit the charismatic definition. A slight majority of all born again Christians (51%) is charismatic. Nearly half of all adults who attend a Protestant church (46%) are charismatic.

This is fascinating information! For far too long, the charismatic community of faith has been viewed as some kind of fringe-group that operates outside the bounds of orthodox Christendom. As stated by the Barna report, "Pentecostal or charismatic Christianity is viewed by some Americans as an emotional, theologically suspect form of the Christian faith." The report goes on to say that the charismatic community has traditionally been considered as, "a very vocal and visible, but numerically small slice of the grand religious pie in the United States."

However, it appears that the winds of change are blowing and by the power of the Holy Spirit, the tide is turning. More and more evangelical Christians are beginning to understand, accept and appreciate the vital role and function that the charismatic community has played in the church today. I believe the constant growth of the charismatic community should be considered as proof of God's plan for us in end-time ministry. Part of that function has been the process of unification, where by, the charismatic community continues to "endeavor to keep the unity of the Spirit in the bond of peace." In fact, it is a function that reaches across racial and continental divides, penetrates beyond social and economic barriers, and unites Christians across just about every line of denominational affiliation.

Again, the information from The Barna Group certainly confirms what I have observed over the past twenty years. The results of that pursuit represent still another trend in the Christian landscape at home and abroad. The nature of the charismatic relationship to the traditional church is changing from a non-denominational, to an interdenominational relationship within the body of Christ.

United in the Future of Faith

Given the nature and affects of the changes occurring within the charismatic community, it is clear that it will never be again as it once was, just as Minister Martin has said. If indeed this is true, then where do we go from here? Considering the fact that our bright and sunny view of the charismatic Christian beach has been jaded by the reality and casualties of spiritual warfare, and the improprieties of a few influential figures; we must ask ourselves what the future holds for the charismatic Christian movement.

During my interview with Pastor McMiller, I asked what kind of changes he has noticed regarding the charismatic community and what he believed GOD may be doing in end-time ministry. He mentioned three specific areas of interest that are pertinent to our community of faith. The first area that he addressed was the search for truth among church laity. "I see a growing hunger for truth and solid biblical teaching among laity. As a result, that hunger has created a situation where the tale is wagging the dog, so to speak, where laity has begun to drive the pursuit for truth. Part of the reason for this situation is the greater availability of other sources and resources that teach the truth of GOD's word. That increased availability of truth causes people to challenge the pastor's teachings that are not scripturally correct."

Secondly, this has led to something else Pastor McMiller has seen within charismatic circles. He has noticed a growing trend toward embracing more fundamental evangelical teaching. "I see an exodus out of some of the traditional churches, where it is strictly emotional and 'charismatic only' in nature. Which has produced an exodus into some other ministries (of other persuasions), where the truth is being taught." However, McMiller thinks that there is a paradigm shift taking place among church leadership. "Therefore," he says, "Pastors are waking up and saying, 'We've got to do something, because we don't want to lose the people!' Leaders are realizing that they have been wrong about certain teachings and directions. They are realizing there is more to this than the traditional aspect. We also have to look at the fact that certain ministries are falling; strong charismatic ministries that are falling and coming up with strange doctrines. It makes you look at it and ask, 'Well, what does the word say?'."

The third area of interest that Pastor McMiller addressed was the issue of idolatry within the church. He said, "We have idolized certain teachings and traditions within the church, and I don't kick people over traditions, but when you make traditions your focus, then you are in error. As a point of reference, McMiller recalled the biblical account of Moses and the bronze serpent, as an example of idolatry. In the account found in Numbers 21:7-9, God used the bronze serpent as an instrument to bring salvation and deliverance, but later the people began to worship the bronze serpent and turned it into an instrument of idolatry. In 2Kings 18:4 we read, *"...for until those days the children of Israel burned incense to it and called it Nehushtan."*

McMiller then said, "Now, that was GOD's command to Moses to do that, but that was just for that season and period. But they kept that brazen serpent and pole and turned it into idolatry and GOD brought judgment on them later on. So even though GOD spoke here, His voice moved. We can't just rally around something God spoke in history and make that the cornerstone and centerpiece of what we believe, because GOD is on the move! He moves and keeps going, therefore, we must move with Him." Unfortunately, this is what we have done within the body of Christ; that includes both the traditional evangelical and the charismatic communities. But we must be willing to do exactly what king Hezekiah did when it says, "He removed the high place and broke the sacred pillars, cut down the wooden images and broke in pieces the bronze serpent that Moses had made."

Pastor McMiller continued by saying, "We have idolized a lot of people! We have put them on pedestals and I see GOD shaking the pedestals, because we can't fixate on people." Therefore, GOD is shaking the body of Christ to get our eyes off of people, and even certain teachings, where we have just fixated on that teaching. That includes prosperity or whatever, where we have idolized any one element and left out all the rest, then you're wrong. So, GOD is shaking some things. Even our economy is being shaken. Everything that can be shaken will be shaken, so that we can get our eyes off of certain things and elements and people, and get our eyes on Him. I think He's getting our eyes back on Jesus Christ, because the bottom line is, it's all about Him."

In light of the fact that GOD is on the move and that He appears to be shaking things up all around us, I asked Pastor McMiller where he thought GOD might be leading His people. And to my surprise, his response was quite optimistic. As he addressed the fourth and final trend he has noticed, he said "I think GOD is getting the body ready for this next move. And Tim, I wish I could tell you what that move is, but I just know GOD is doing something. He's bringing the body of Christ together.

I see certain events designed to bring the body of Christ together. Where there used to be a divide, I see a coming together around Him. Not around a teaching, not around a person, but around Jesus Christ. So I see a lot of ministries that are coming together for events, such as Mega-fest, where men and pastors from various denominations are coming together. And I'm not speaking about the ecumenical movement that some want to see where the Muslims and the Christians and everybody says "we're all one." I still believe in absolutes. I still believe that Jesus Christ is the Way! But I believe within the body of Christianity, people with their labels are coming together you know, and blurring the denominational divide. So I can see that the walls are coming down."

Pastor Willie McMiller's comments and observations rang with truth as they bore witness with what I too believe GOD is doing in these last days. Again, Jesus prayed, "Make them one even as We are one." It is true that we do not know exactly what GOD is doing, but we can recognize certain patterns from the history of mankind and from the word of GOD. And the pattern that we should recognize is that His word will surely come to pass. Indeed, this "coming together" is not the ecumenical movement that some have taught. However, the spirit behind the ecumenical movement that we see taking place within Christendom, I believe that is GOD. And He is trying to unify His people through the ministry of the charismatic community.

The Church Goes Off Road

In light of these sobering issues, not everyone's prognostication about the future the Charismatic Church is as bright and optimistic. When Dr. Conny was asked about the future of the ministry in end-time events, her response was both surprising and sobering. After a moment of explaining the difficulty in trying to answer such a question, she responded by saying, "I'm not sure that the Charismatic Church will survive." Of course I was completely blown away by her answer. After quickly getting past the initial shock, asked her to please elaborate upon her response. She said, "That's only because I know that God spoke a word to me a couple of years back (maybe five years ago), and God said, "I'm going to take the Church off road." As a matter of fact, I believe that there is going to be a decline in church (attendance) period. And that the church will be the actual individuals, rather than your organized bodies."

Dr. Conny then began to mention some of the negative trends that are taking place across the Christian landscape. She explains, "People are leaving the church in droves. Pastors are quitting and closing their doors, and saying, 'I'm sick of this!' And its not that they are sick of God, but they are sick of the church politics and they're sick of what they are seeing. That's because church is no longer about the original design, it's like a million years from that. I don't think the church (both charismatic and traditional evangelical churches), as it is now, is going to survive in that state."

She went on to explain further, about how she believes that there will still be churches, but they will no longer be the authoritative voice anymore. "The authoritative voice is going to be off road." In her explanation of what she meant by off road, she adds, "You know when you take a jeep off road you get off the main street. You get into the woods and the rocks, well the miracles are no longer going to happen in the churches. The miracles are going to happen in the streets somewhere. Somewhere under the viaducts, somewhere in the hospitals where the layperson, which is really in love with God and sees somebody suffering, lays their hands (upon the sick for the Lord to raise them up, through the prayer of faith). It's going to be off road. More and more people are leaving the church, and I can't blame them!" Taking the opportunity to interject, I ask the question, "So when you say, 'off road', you mean out of mainstream?" Without a pause, she replied "Out of mainstream most certainly. And even out of the building! And even out of the building (as she reiterated to underscore her point)."

Dr. Conny is not alone in her dire description of the current state and pending demise of the institutional Church as we know it. Again, to cite the work of Christian sociologist George Barna from his book entitled *The Second Coming of the Church: a Blueprint for Survival*, Barna opens the very first chapter by say, "Let's CUT TO THE CHASE. After nearly two decades of studing Christian churches in America, I'm convinced that the typical church as we know it today has a rapidly expiring shelf life." Barna reiterates his prognosis by saying, "At the risk of sounding like an alarmist, I believe the Church in America has no more than five years– perhaps even less – to turn itself around and begin to affect the culture, rather than be affected by it." Barna then notes the reasons for the dilemma, "Because our culture completely reinvents itself every three to five years, and people are intensely seeking spiritual direction, and our central moral and spiritual trends are engulfed in a downward spiral, we have no more than a half-decade to turn things around."

As the author-analyst continues his analysis of the situation, he writes "The world around us is changing at an unprecedented pace... Most American churches, however, are holding fast to programs and goals established by their charter members years ago. Many of these ministries have mastered the art of denying the cataclysmic cultural changes around them, responding with cosmetic changes that make little difference." To compound the problem, Barna notes the fact that Christians act and behave no different than the unbelievers we are trying to reach. As a result, the church in America is incapable of responding to the present moral crisis. Fortunately, George Barna offers a glimmering ray of hope. He uses the anaolgy of an oil tanker as he proposes that it is possible to turn the ship around. "In order for this to happen, however," Barna says, "...we must respond strategically- and pray like we've never prayed before."

If Dr. Conny Williams and George Barna are correct in their prediction, the road to recovery and relevance will be marked by trying times and difficult decision ahead. The face of ministry, in this modern age of Christianity, will look very different than in the past. This could explain why some other trends are taking place within the body of Christ. For example, the rise and popularity of something called, "the Emerging Church movement", which in many ways echoes the early days of the Charismatic Movement. Many believers are forsaking the traditional confines of a church building and are choosing rather to gather in homes, public parks and in other non-traditional spaces. Shepherds are choosing to pastor and preach from their homes, rather than from the pulpit of a traditional sanctuary. In fact, not only does it remind me of the early day of the Charismatic Movement, but it also mirrors the early days of Christianity as people, both Jews and gentiles, gathered from house to house for prayer and worship.

Please understand that I am not supporting the abandonment of the institution of the traditional church by advocating such activities. Nor am I trying to say that we can know what the next great move of God will be. But as Barna points out, we must be willing to change if we want to remain relevant and influential to the culture around us. Therefore, my goal is to point out some of the trends I have personal encountered that are changing the face of Christianity as we know it! While such activities may not fit the model for church today, they most certainly are consistent with the biblical record we find in scripture. And while we may not agree on whether are not it is a move of God, one thing is for sure, and that is the fact that more often than not, God's plans and ways do not always correspond with what we consider orthodox. I believe that such changes are motivated by the Holy Spirit, in an attempt to bring the members of the body of Christ back to what church is really supposed to be about and to get away from everything that has become so religiously institutional about the church.

A Future Remnant in the Faith

Another interesting perspective arose during my discussion with Pastor Femi when I asked him about the future of the Charismatic Church. We talked about the course of direction that many charismatic ministries have taken and if it is too late to turn the proverbial ship around. Through the thick Nigerian accent again came an interesting and insightful response. He said, "There is always a remnant. There are always people who have not bowed the knee. There are always folks who are sincerely seeking to find the purposes of God.

Some guys are just a bunch of clowns who are basically trying to do their own thing. But at the same time, the nature of God is that He always has a remnant. And that remnant always bows the knee to Him. So even in the Word of Faith and Charismatic Movement, there are some ministers and pastors who are going to come out of it and say, "Well not to judge you or criticize you, but this is not for us." There was a time where I come from when if you were not charismatic you were going to hell. For everybody else who did not speak in tongues, they were going to hell. But I for one look at that and say there is a problem with that! The Bible says if you believe and if you confess, you will be saved. And that's all! I can't add to it and I can't take from that.

Now believing in Jesus; believing in Mary does not remove or take away from believing in Jesus. It's an extra that I think there are problems with, but the fundamentals are there. Nobody is perfect! And I think the Word of Faith and Charismatic Movement are going to come to that place where some people are going to rise up and say, "Enough!" And I think there are folks who are there already, but it hasn't reached the critical mass. But I think that it's ok, because if it becomes too loud, then it becomes another "move." And once it becomes another move, then it too starts to look for legitimacy. It starts to establish itself and the leaders of it start to look for recognition. They start to think, saying "We are the ones!" You know…"We are on the cutting edge…we know the mind of God for now!" And then that becomes another movement. And then it becomes another monument…and then we've got problem again. So I think there is always a remnant that God will use. And when this movement, when its cup is full, then it will pass. But I think for right now, there are a lot of folks who are still speaking the truth."

1 Chronicles 12:32 tells us that the son of Issachar, *"...had understanding of the times, to know what Israel ought to do."* We too should be wise in our understanding of the times we live in. If we are going to be effective in our efforts to fulfill the Great Commission through end-time ministry, then we must consider the impact and meaning of these various trends upon the church. Everything from the reintroduction of the gift of tongues and the charismatic gifts, to the interdenominational activity and ecumenical movement within the denominational ranks of the church; and even the move to get the church outside the building and into the highways and byways of the streets, is all happening under the careful guidance of the Holy Spirit and the control of God Almighty Himself. Therefore, we must be mindful of message and ministry of the Holy Spirit in these changing times.

This was exactly the point that was made in an interview I had with another pastor and minister, who was visiting minister from the United Kingdom of Europe. Dr. Sola Fola-Alade is the pastor of Trinity Chapel in London, England. Dr. Sola initially trained as a medical physician, but after becoming a Christian, he went on to study at the London Bible Institute. He serves as a fulltime pastor under the Redeemed Church of God, a Pentecostal affiliated denomination, which began in 1952. As pastor, he shepherds a congregation of over one thousand members, and is the author of a number of books and publisher of one of Europe's most contemporary, international, values based magazine publications.

When I heard that Dr. Sola Fola-Alade would be speaking at an African Nigerian church in the St. Louis area, where a friend of mine attended, I quickly asked if an interview could be arranged. A couple of weeks later, after Dr. Sola had arrived, my friend called to say that the pastor of the host church had called and said that my request for an interview had been granted. It was scheduled for the following Sunday morning, immediately following the service; needless to say, I took advantage of the opportunity.

My wife and I had visited the church before, on several different occasions, and always enjoyed the service. It is one of those examples of a charismatic blend, with an African, international flavor that combines the spirited feel of lively African harmonies and beats, with familiar contemporary worship and praise songs. And the teaching is always refreshing and challenging. The message from the guest speaker from London, England was no different. After the service, Pastor Femi who is the pastor of the host church, asked us to join Dr. Sola in the pastor's study. After a formal introduction and some cordial conversation, I turned on the recorder and we were ready to begin.

One of the first questions I asked Dr. Sola was about the impact and influence of the charismatic church upon his denomination. He explained that, "From its inception in 1952, the Redeemed Church of God was born out of a charismatic experience." According to Dr. Sola, the original founder was a Nigerian illiterate, who received a vision of the name of the church (Redeemed Church of God) in a dream. The interesting aspect about the vision is that the name appeared to be written upon a blackboard, with words written in the English language. When the Nigerian awoke from the dream, he wrote down the letters he saw in the vision and began to seek out someone that could tell him the meaning of the unfamiliar script. After finding someone who was able to read the script he had written down from the dream, he was informed that the message was in the English tongue, which read Redeemed Church of God. Of course, this was a fascinating story, and I knew that it was just a prelude of what was to come during our interview!

As I sat in the brightly lit study, accompanied by my wife, Dr. Conny (the friend who invited me) and Pastor Femi, I asked Dr. Sola about the state of the church in Europe and what was God doing in the Christian community there in London? Dr. Sola explained, "The spiritual landscape in Europe had become very dark, so much so that if you mention God in the streets, people will stop and look at you, because it has become very secular there. Twenty years ago, the church was essentially dead because of a decline in church attendance in the larger, traditional churches that originally began in Europe." He said that the churches started by people like Charles Spurgeon, John Wesley and William Booth, were virtually empty. These large edifices only see an average attendance between six and forty visitors a week. That was absolutely astounding to hear!

However, he said that when the Nigerian African Christian community began to come to Europe, "They brought God with them and that was the beginning of a turn-about for the Christian community in Europe. In the past ten to fifteen years, we have seen a dramatic increase in church attendance." However, Dr. Sola noted that the increase is not among the former traditional churches, but rather among that are considered to be Pentecostal or charismatic in beliefs. "For instance, in the Redeemed Church of God, I have seen my church grow from six members to over a thousand in the past few years. I am also the overseer of eight other churches. And another minister there, who started with twelve people, has seen his congregation grow to twelve thousand members. This is the kind of growth we are seeing as a result of the move of the Holy Spirit across Europe."

As with each of my other interviewees, I asked Dr. Sola Fola-Alade what his thoughts were regarding the future role of the charismatic church in end-time ministry. Up to this point in our discussion, he had been extremely generous in his patience and attention, and I could see that he was spent after preaching and teaching prior to our interview. Therefore, with patience wearing thin, he kindly said, "If I may be honest with you, it's not about denominations for me. It is about the work of the Holy Spirit, which began in the book of Acts, and continues to this day. So whenever God wants to speak to the church, God sends a man with a message. From that message, the Holy Spirit starts a movement. But when that movement becomes a monument, then by the power of the Holy Spirit, God sends a 'breakout man' with another message to begin another movement."

Dr. Sola continued to chronicle the major movements in Christianity by saying, "Just like Jesus sent Peter, Paul and the other apostles, with the message of the gospel, which started the Christian movement. Paul's message to the gentiles of Rome started the Christian movement that became the Catholic Church of western civilization. But after the Catholic movement became a monument, He sent Martin Luther with a message, and through the Holy Spirit the Protestant movement brought reformation. One hundred years later, the Holy Spirit sent John Wesley with a message that started the Methodist movement. When the Methodist became too methodical, the Holy Spirit sent other men who broke away from the monument. On and on until He sent William Seymour and Charles Parham with the Pentecostal message, from which, the Pentecostal movement was born. Now, from the Pentecostal Movement, came the Charismatic Movement."

At the end of my interview with Dr. Sola Fola-Alade, he concluded our discussion by saying, "In my opinion, the Charismatic Movement has been the most influential and phenomenal movement of our time. As I said, I'm not into the denominational thing, but it's possible that the Charismatic Movement has also become a monument. I'm not sure, but we need to be careful about that, because it is not about what the Charismatic Church is doing. It should always be about what the Holy Spirit wants to do through the body of Christ. And that is what I see." Of course, I appreciated Dr. Sola's insightful, yet poignant comments, which reminded me of the very reason for this book. It is not my intention to spot light the work of the Charismatic Movement, but rather to emphasize the work of the Holy Spirit through the charismatic community.

Contemplating a Charismatic Future

As I talked with Dr. Sola, I couldn't help but to think about the fact that Christianity had been at the center of European culture for so many years. But the slow erosion of Christian values and moral standards have declined to such a degree that the culture has all but rejected its Christian heritage. The most sobering aspect of Dr. Sola's comments about the spiritual state of the U.K. was how much it reminded me of America and the direction in which we are headed as a nation.

Once again, as Christians, we are facing the winds of change. Right now, even as the pages of this book are being penned, the American people are facing another pivotal point in our nation's history. Issues such as same sex marriage and partial birth abortion are ripping at the moral fabric of our country. Ethical questions regarding embryonic stem cell and cloning research make the headline news on a daily basis. Efforts to pass laws that would make preaching the Word of God and spreading the message of the gospel a hate crime are being fought on every legislative and legal front, while attempts to wipe away all vestiges of the Christian faith from the public arena, present a constant threat to our fundamental rights and liberties. To say it plainly, we are at war for the very soul of our nation!

To their credit, the evangelical Christian community has been very instrumental in taking a stand against these attacks upon the body of Christ and our nation. However, they can't do it alone.

But by the same token, they have done very little to reach across the table of debate, for the purpose of joining forces with members and leaders of the charismatic Christian community. Instead, many Evangelicals and certain apologetic leaders seem to practice a kind of theologically intellectual elite religious separation that is based upon questionable biblical biases and debatable differences of doctrine. Beloved, this ought not to be! Such attitudes and actions are in error to say the least and are inappropriate behavior for children of the Most High God and members of the body of Christ. They seem to believe that the members and leaders of the charismatic community have nothing to offer the body of Christ.

However, the good news is God is in control and He has a plan and purpose for the Word of Faith message and the Charismatic Church in the end-time. It is high time for the charismatic community to get involved in the fight for the kingdom of heaven. That's not to say that we have not been involved as Christian soldiers, but in light of our focus and recent reputation within the body of Christ, we must ask ourselves what we have been fighting for. Let's face it! By comparison to other Christians around the world, as American Christians in the Catholic Church (universal community of faith), God has blessed us with plenty of the riches and blessings of His goodness. We've gotten the money, the houses, the cars and all the prosperity we could ever imagine and we are left with the question, "What now?" Therefore in these last days we must begin to look beyond ourselves to see the bigger picture in God's wonderful plan for end time ministry.

As we join forces with our evangelical brothers and sisters in the body of Christ to do the work of the ministry, I believe that together, we can again walk in the model for ministry that was first delivered to the saints. We become ministers of the gospel who are able to exercise both the wisdom of reason in the Spirit, and the demonstrative power of the Spirit. This is an amazing opportunity that we have before us; it is to fulfill the prayer of Jesus in John 17, and to be the true body of Christ for end time miracles in ministry. This opportunity represents a perfect picture of the dual aspect of the ministry of Jesus.

Just as the gospel was proclaimed by the Angel of the Lord at the beginning of the Church, it is that same message of good news and glad tidings that is preached and proclaimed by every member of the body of the body of Christ, including the charismatic community. That message is *"For God so loved the world that He gave his only begotten Son... (John 3:16)"*. In John 1:1, 14, Jesus is called *"the word that was made flesh, and dwelt among men"*. And in Hebrews 4:12, the word of God is likened to a *two-edge sword,* in its application of the truth.

This passage exemplifies the pattern that God uses to communicate His message of love and redemption to us. It is a dual approach, double-edge application of Christ's method of ministry, as both Savior and Lord. His truth is presented to the world as a collective offer of redemption as well as an individual invitation for salvation. In short, Jesus came and died as Savior of the world, but rose to live again as the personal Lord and Savior of every one that receives Him. Therefore, lets apply this dual approach as we look at God's will and word for the charismatic community and the massage of faith in the years to come; first individually, then collectively.

Cultivating Faith for the End Time

In the book of Luke 18:1-8, Jesus gives a parable about persistence in prayer through faith. In the parable we find a judge who has no regard for God or man. Next, we are introduced to a widow who is so persistent in her efforts to solicit help from the judge that the he is compelled to grant her request. In verse five the unjust judge said, *"…because this widow troubles me I will avenge her, lest by her continual coming she weary me."* Notice in verse six of the passage that Jesus instructs His listeners to "Hear what the unjust judge said" in the previous verse. Jesus then makes a profound comparison as

He declares that God will most certainly do the same for His own elect who demonstrate the same tenacity as the proverbial widow. Finally, Jesus asks a very interesting and disconcerting question. In verse eight of the parable, Jesus said *"...Nevertheless, when the Son of Man comes, will He really find faith on the earth?"* Why would Jesus ask such a question?

Well according to the book of Romans 12:3, God has given every believer a measure of faith. We can logically conclude that in the parable of the unjust judge and the widow, He is not referring to saving faith or the kind of faith that simply believes in His existence. Therefore, He must be alluding to a deeper level of faith. Hebrews 11:6 gives us the corroborating answer as we read *"But without faith it is impossible to please Him, for he who comes to God must believe that He is, and that He is a rewarder of those who diligently seek Him."* We are to serve as members in particular and collectively in accordance with the measure we have been given. It is that capacity to demonstrate faith that is persistent and undaunted in nature that Jesus encourages us to develop.

The kind of faith mentioned in this passage is the kind that is cultivated over time and stimulated by opposition. This is exactly the kind of faith that the charismatic community has been groomed by God to communicate and demonstrate in these last days. Again, this is the purpose for the message and ministry of the Word of Faith for the end time. No longer is it just about getting our needs met, but it is about helping to cultivate, motivate and stimulate the rest of our brothers and sisters to believe God for the promise.

What promise you ask? For that answer, we must refer again to our text, which instructs us to hear and understand what the unjust judge has said in verse five. The Jesus asks, "And shall not God avenge his own elect who cry out day and night to Him, though He bears long with them? This is where that tenacious kind of faith will be instrumental in encouraging the members of the body of Christ to believe that Jesus will return to avenge His people, despite the end-time opposition that we face.

It is in that time, when perilous times will come, and when men become lovers of themselves rather than lovers of God. The Bible tells us that the day will come when the anti-Christ will make war against the saints to prevail against them. That is when the message of faith that believes the promise will be more necessary than ever. It will be during the days when the pages of the Revelation are revealed that we must be ready to preach the Word of Faith for the end time. That is why we must begin to sharpen our side of the proverbial sword, by sharpening the focus of our role and ability within the body of Christ.

Healing for the End Time

The proclamation of healing is an important part of the ministry of the Word of Faith in the end time. And this is the measure of faith that has been given to the charismatic community. As a contributing member in the body of Christ, we must continue to preach and teach the portion God has gifted us to deliver. We must continue to encourage people to have faith in GOD, just as Jesus encouraged the first disciples of the church. The GOD that Jesus spoke about is the same God, who from the Old Testament said, "I am the GOD that heals thee". And He is the very same One who sent His word to the children of Israel and healed their diseases. Jesus is the same Christ who walked the streets of Jerusalem and went about healing all who were sick and oppressed. Since Jesus demonstrated that healing was part of His New Testament ministry, and the GOD of the Old Testament has said that He is the same yesterday, today and forever. Then He is still the God that heals!

As ministers of the gospel of Jesus Christ, we must continue to proclaim His message of healing in today's church. We must continue to teach people how to receive their healing and how to walk and live in divine health and wellness. Upon His return, Jesus will be looking for folks who believe Him to be the One who comes with healing in His wings. Therefore collectively, it is up to members who believe that He is still the Great Physician, to keep preaching and teaching the possibility and promise of divine health and wellness until He returns with healing for the nations.

Miracles for the End Time

Our God is the God of miracles and He still desires to intervene and interact in the lives and affairs of mankind. In the book of Daniel, the writer declares, *"the people who know their God shall be strong and do exploits."* Remember that this is a book that speaks directly to end-time events. Consider also that Jesus tells His disciples **"and these signs shall follow them that believe. In My name they shall..."** Shall what? Do exploits such as heal the sick and cast out demons, and if necessary, even raise the dead! Jesus went on to tell them in another passage that they would go on to do even greater works than He, because He had to go to the Father.

So what was Jesus saying? Simply that He was available to God, as the Son of God, to be used by God to do the improbable, impossible and the miraculous will of God. His message to His disciples, and to the believers then and now, was that we too must make ourselves available to God through Christ, to be used as earthen vessels for miracles in the earth. God is still looking for people who will believe Him for that which seems improbable and impossible. The message of miraculous faith to believe God is still relevant for the end-time church.

God is still looking for water walking, mountain moving and praying prison-breaking earth shaking disciples. His eyes are still looking throughout the whole earth, searching for those individuals who have a heart that is full of faith and loyalty. Men and women who are exercised and can operate in the gift of faith. When such individuals yield themselves as vessels, through the power of the Holy Spirit, God continues to prove His self strong through signs and wonders.

Christians still need a voice with a message of encouragement affirmation. Therefore, we must continue to preach and proclaim that *"without faith, it is impossible to please God"* and *"nothing is impossible to him that believes."* As the charismatic community, it is part of our on going ministry, to continue to provide a message of maturity for Christians to operate in the gifts of the Spirit and to provide and atmosphere of faith that allows the Holy Spirit to move freely when the gifts are in operation. We must continue to offer a basis for education and instruction in the gifts of the Spirit, for leaders and lay-members in the five fold ministry. *This is necessary "for the perfecting of the saints, for the work of the ministry, until we all..."* Because when He returns, He will be looking for believers who are full of faith and looking for the miracle of His coming! So then, we are to continue to proclaim that He is the God of miracles, until He returns.

Faith in the Future of Israel

Finally, as we consider the role of the charismatic church in God's end time plan for mankind, we must again acknowledge His will and promise for the people of Israel. Contrary to the opinion based upon Replacement Theology that some choose to subscribe to, God has not forsaken His people. In Genesis 12:1-3, the word of God is clear to Abraham regarding the future of his descendents when God said, *"I will make you a great nation; I will bless you and make your name great; and you shall be a blessing. I will bless those who bless you, and I will curse him who curses you; and in you all the families of the earth shall be blessed."* Since we know that God's word does not change and that He is not a man that he should lie, nor the son of man that He should repent, then we can safely say that this promise is still in effect. Therefore, it is up to us to decide whether or not we are going to be a part of what the God of Israel is doing in these last days, as it pertains to the Jewish people and the land of Israel.

While some may argue that the timing of the 1967 recapturing of Jerusalem and the birth of the Charismatic Movement are purely coincidental, I believe that the Jewish/Charismatic connection is more than happenstance. From its inception, the charismatic community has been instrumental in seeking to aid in the restoration and fulfillment of God's word concerning the people of Israel. And that connection is very much alive and well in today's charismatic community and the church at large as thousands of believer stand in prayerful support for the nation of Israel.

Embracing Our Hebraic Roots

One of the most exciting trends that I have noticed taking place within the charismatic community is a gradual embrace of the Jewish people, the Hebrew language and the teachings of the Torah. It appears that God is turning the heart of the Christian Church back to its Judean birthright and Hebraic heritage. I mentioned early on how it became sheik to speak Greek as the charismatic community developed and appreciation and affection for original Greek words related to biblical study. In the same way, there is a very real and genuine appreciation developing for Jewish teachings and traditions as they relate to Christ the Messiah and His second coming. Interest in the Torah, the appointed feast and festivals, and archeology in the Holy Land, have all increased over the past few years.

There seems to be a divine paradigm shift taking place that is moving us away from the traditional Western perspective if Christianity established by the Greek-Eurocentric Christian

Church; back to a more Hebraic foundation for understanding the scriptures. In most instances, it's not a question of whether or not western Christianity is wrong about its approach to scripture. But rather it is a question of original intent. Western Christianity's understanding is sometimes incomplete, misconstrued or redefined. This new Hebraic approach is not meant to replace what we already know about the scriptures, but is intended to supplement and enrich our current understanding. Therefore, the affect of this shift is re-evaluation, revitalization and a reshaping of our Christian thinking.

Remember, Jesus was Jewish and so were the original founding fathers of the Christian faith. It stands to reason then that we can learn a thing or two from our Jewish brothers and sisters in Christ. As we acquire a better understanding of the God of the Torah, through a rediscovery of our Hebraic roots, it produces a greater appreciation for the Jewish heritage and legacy that was originally left to the early Christian Church by Jesus Christ and the twelve Apostles.

I have personally experienced this transition and growing appreciation within my own life as a Christian. It began with a trip to the museum a few years ago when I had the opportunity to see an exhibit called "Treasures from the Lost Tombs of Ur." The exhibition featured a lecture by Dr. John Russell who spoke on "A New Look at the Ancient Kingdom of Ur," during his visit at the St. Louis

Art Museum. The exhibit also featured artifacts excavated at the city
of Ur by archeologist from a joint University of Pennsylvania and
British Museum expedition during the1920's. The thing that made
the experience so interesting and exciting for me is the fact that they
made mention of the biblical patriarch Abraham. Of course, I knew
the story of Abraham was true because the word of God is true, but
the archeology and artifacts brought the Jewish patriarch to life in
a way that literally opened my eyes to a whole new world of biblical
history and understanding. It caused the scriptures to come alive in
a way that was relevant and personal to me.

The next example of God's divine instruction and direction was
presented via a chance meeting with Dr. Conny, which gave me the
opportunity to take a course called *"The Jewishness of Jesus."* We have
some friends who are Messianic believers and we wanted to get a
better understanding of the prayers and practices introduced to us
by those friends. When my wife and I ran into Dr. Conny at a local
restaurant, she mentioned that she would be teaching a class about
the Jewish heritage of Christianity. The funny thing was that Kim
and I had just talked earlier that day, about taking a class on that
very same subject. Of course, we recognized the divine hand of fate
and took advantage of the opportunity for education. The class was
extremely informative and exciting, but most of all, it really gave

us a greater understanding of scripture from the Jewish perspective, and a new found appreciation for the biblical history of the Jewish people.

As I look around at what God is doing in the body of Christ, more and more, I see how He is stirring the hearts of believers to give them a love and interest in the land of Israel. Christian television is expanding to include televised charismatic Christian conferences broadcasted from Israel. More and more Christian organizations are taking part in tours that visit the land of Israel. And possibly, one of the most vivid examples of the Christian change of heart toward Israel was demonstrated during a Papal visit to the Holy Land by Pope John Paul II. His gesture of love and proclamation of unity was historic and unprecedented in its implications. It signaled an end to the long standing rift between Roman Catholic Christianity and historic Jewish Monotheism. Yes, the divorce of Christianity from Judaism was finally coming to an end.

So what's the reason for this sudden change of heart concerning Israel? Why are people so interested in the events of the Middle East? I believe it is because of end-time events foretold in the book of Zechariah, regarding the fate and future of Israel. In Zechariah 12:1-3 God says of Israel, *"The burden of the word of the LORD against Israel. Thus says the LORD…Behold, I will make Jerusalem a cup of drunkenness to all the surrounding peoples, when they lay siege against Judah and Jerusalem. And it shall happen in that day that I will make Jerusalem a very heavy stone for all peoples; all who would heave it away will surely be cut in pieces, though all nations of the earth are gathered against it."*

Prior to the shift of church authority from Jerusalem to Rome, Jerusalem was considered the center of the world regarding religious worship, and the focus of trade and commerce was centered in the Middle East. According to the scripture, the world's attention will once again be turned to Jerusalem. Therefore, I believe that the turning of the heart of the Church toward Israel directly corresponds with the shift of the worlds attention back to Jerusalem.

Remember, God has promised to deliver and vindicate the nation of Israel, at the end of the Battle of Armageddon. Therefore the security of Israel's future is still part of God's end time plan. He has also promise that all the nations of the world will travel to a resurrected temple in Israel to worship Christ during His millennial reign; therefore, Jerusalem will once again become the center of worship for the world. God has said that this specific region of the world would become the chosen geographic site for the New Jerusalem, which will descend from heaven to earth. Despite the claims of some proponents of replacement theology, it is still all about Israel and the city of Jerusalem.

As Christians begin to understand certain concepts of Jewish practices and customs, and what they were intended to reveal to us about the nature of the relationship and ministry of Christ to the Church, then we are able to appreciate the significance of Jewish teachings and traditions. For example, The Feast of Trumpets, the Day of Atonement and the Feast of Tabernacles are all intended to reveal truths about the first and second coming Messiah. There is a prophetic element within the feast that is meant to prepare us for what is to come. When one studies the details of Jewish practices regarding marriage, the wedding feast and the consummation, one will literally find layers of truth that all point to the Messiah, His ministries to the Church and His coming. Those layers of truth are intended to provide believers with a solid foundation and in-depth understanding of who the Messiah is, what He is to us, and who and what we are to Him. This principle was foundational to the Jewish way of life and their understanding of the Messiah. Jesus knew this fact. That is why He was so hard on the Pharisees in their discussions regarding the signs of His coming (Matthew 16:1-4).

Therefore, to understand the feasts is to understanding what God is about to do in the earth. Such information will be useful in the days ahead as the time of the Great Tribulation draws closer. In Psalms 122:6, we are instructed as believers to "Pray for the peace of Jerusalem." How can we truly fulfill the call and command by God to earnestly pray, without first receiving a heart for ministry for the Jewish people? God is preparing His people to fulfill their call to ministry by turning the heart of Christianity back to the land and people from which it has come.

Ministry of Hebraic Reconciliation

To further illustrate the point and to get a better understanding of this new direction for the Church, I wanted to talk with someone with more experience in this area of ministry. In addition, I wanted to be sure that what I've been sensing and witnessing is an accurate assessment of the perceived situation, so I called upon the expert advice of Dr. Walter Oakley. Dr. Oakley is the co-founder of Beth-El Ministries along with his wife, Dr. Elizabeth Oakley and both are graduates of Midwest Seminary of Bible Theology. Dr. Oakley currently serves a consultant for plans to rebuild the Jewish Temple in Jerusalem. He is also a prolific writer and has written and co-written biblical study courses for several religious schools and organizations, which include American Mission Teams, International College of Bible Theology, Midwest Seminary of Bible Theology and Colorado Theological Seminary. Dr. Walter also operates a website that is focused on educating the general Christian community about "all things Jewish" and how that information is particularly relative to us today as contemporary Christians.

When I contacted Dr. Oakley to ask for his assistance in writing the book, he was more than helpful. Not only was there a certain command of respect present because of the level of expertise and understanding that he possesses about the subject, but there was also a passion and a fire I noticed from the very moment he began to share his own personal testimony. He said, "In the mid 80's I used to go and hang out at the local Christian Book Store. I lived and pastored a small Charismatic Church in Southern California. I would usually show up there on Tuesday afternoons just to hang out. Tuesday evenings several of us would just hang out and many times the Presence of G-d[19] would show up and minister to us in some special way."

"One of the guys that would hang out with us was a Messianic Jew. He suggested we read a book by Vendyl Jones (Endy – Indiana Jones) called "Will the Real Jesus Please Stand." This book opened my eyes to the foundation of the Early Church. Likewise, it gave me a perspective that allowed me to realize that HaShem (G-d) was not finished (and He never had been) with the Jews. Many of the Covenants and Festivals HaShem (G-d) with Yisrael are clearly eternal (Shemot or Exodus 12:14-17)."

"After reading the book," Dr. Oakley said, "I was very troubled. The store owner and I went to see Vendyl Jones at a meeting in Long beach California where he discussed his attempts to find the Ark of the Covenant. At that meeting we found a Rabbi that would travel to our community and teach us the Torah. As you might surmise, it was tough for us because this was an Orthodox Rabbi who did not believe in Yeshua (Jesus)." To my surprise; but quite understandably, Dr. Walter acknowledged that this new information did not come without a price. "I must confess that I had a collapse of faith." as he continued by saying, "I struggled to find my way back. I felt like Neo in the movie 'The Matrix.' I had taken that pill that opened my eyes and would no longer allow me to live with the things that I had been told in my youth. My quest began. I was now on a journey to find the truth. I studied and searched. In those days there were no recourses for studying this ideology. Likewise, there were no contacts to be made with others who believed these truths. The journey was hard and long. It is still one of those things that we have to deal with in the contemporary Church world. I found one contact in Texas many years ago where I could buy books that superficially dealt with the subject. Eventually I met others who shared the same ideals and goals that I did. I taught the "Jewishness of Jesus" in several classes. I taught "Biblical Hebrew, the Foundations of the Church and the Effect of Judaism on Early Believers." In teaching these things I made plenty of mistakes. We had no mentors. We had no one to look to for truth or balance. It was a very hard road. In all that I do I still find this road a very hard path to walk."

I wanted to know what kept him going amid so much opposition, and Dr. Oakley responded by saying, "During the early days of this ministry I had a dream. I saw myself moving through a jungle of green vegetation. This vegetation was so thick that I had to cut it with a machete. I looked behind to see others following. I noticed others doing very much what I was doing. However, they were broadening the path." Oakley was quick to point out, "Please do not think that I think that I am the soul pioneer of these things! I later met Joseph Good and became involved with him and his ministry. Joseph Good is someone I believe to be one of the real pioneers of faith and this contemporary move of G-d with men like Vendyl Jones."

Walter Oakley again confessed, "To this very day I struggle. We try to remain balanced yet tell the truth. However, many people do not want to hear the truth. This is because the truth is costly. Rather than remain in the bliss of Christian utopian ideologies we are forced into the reality of Biblical truth. We have come to realize that we are gladly God's slaves." As we discussed the problem of rejection and misunderstanding of the Hebraic Root by the Church, I wanted to know what Dr. Oakley thought might be the main cause for this response by the Church. Dr. Oakley said, "Contemporary Christianity has embraced a Neo-Marcion theology[20]. These things must be overcome and reversed if we are to be the spotless bride that Yeshua will return for. We must also realize that the analogies given in the Scriptures are based on Jewish ideologies and Midrashim. This includes the ideology of the "Bride" of Meshiach. The Bride that Yeshua will return for will be Jewish or a convert (Read the book of Rut {Ruth})." The Neo-Marcion theology that Dr. Oakley spoke of has been embraced by both traditional and charismatic Christians alike.

But the good news is there is a ray of light shining through the proverbial clouds of gloom. Dr. Oakley noted, "However, I have seen the Church world turn towards this movement in the past decade with phenomenal momentum. I believe that this is based on several Scriptures. My wife and I attended a "Basic Judaism" course about 13 years ago. We were the only Gentiles in a vast sea of Jewish attendants. A couple of years ago we decided to take a refresher course on Basic Judaism. This time we were amazed! This time the attendance was predominantly Gentile. Over 85% of the attendants were Gentile. We were forced to ask the simple question: Why?"

Dr. Oakley then began to quote a passage from Zechariah 8:20 which says, *"Thus says the Lord of host: Peoples shall yet come, the inhabitants of many cities; 21 the inhabitants of one city shall go to another, saying, "Come, let us go to entreat the favor of the Lord, and to seek the Lord of host; I myself am going." 22 Many peoples and strong nations shall come to seek the L-rd of hosts in Jerusalem, and to entreat the favor of the Lord. 23 Thus says the Lord of host: In those days ten men from nations of every language shall take hold of a Jew, grasping the hem of his garment and saying, "Let us go with you, for we have heard that G-d is with you."*

He then began again by saying, "This passage has a wealth of things that do not appear in the English translations. Nevertheless, I believe that this prophesy is relevant for our time. I believe that it embodies much of what we are seeing with regards to the move of HaShem in this time. The phrase "ten men of the nations" is of particular importance. It deals with the fact that "ten men" – congregation of Gentiles will become Torah observant. Another point of interest is that the phrase "take hold" is actually repeated in the Hebrew text. We are told by some scholars that this refers to two occurrences that it would have in history. The first occurrence took place just after the time of Yeshua when the Gentile world embraced Judaism in and through Yeshua. Scholars suggest that the second occurrence is relevant to this time that we live in. This is because we are beginning to see a new embracing of the Hebrew Heritage or Roots of our faith. The "grasping the hem of the Jew's garment" is indicative of the Tallit. The Tallit is a symbol of Torah observance. Likewise, the phrase, "Let us go with you, for we have heard that G-d is with you" is indicative of living a Jewish lifestyle."

As he began to wrap up the interview, Dr. Walter Oakley defined the purpose his ministry. "Beth-El Ministries is a ministry that is aimed at taking the fear out of this walk and relationship. We have nothing to fear and everything to gain. Likewise, Beth-El Ministries is aimed at breaking down the wall of partition that Yeshua broke down during his life and Ministry (Ephesians 2:15) Ephesians 2:14-16 reads, "14 *For He Himself is our peace, who made both groups into one and broke down the barrier of the dividing wall,* 15 *by abolishing in His flesh the enmity, which is the Law of commandments contained in ordinances, so that in Himself He might make the two into one new man, thus establishing peace,* 16 *and might reconcile them both in one body to G-d through the cross, by it having put to death the enmity.*"

The word "Law" of verse 15 is dogma in Greek. Dogma is a man made decree. This does not refer to the Commandments dictated by

God to Moshe (Moses). Dogma is a set of rules in addition to the rules of God. So what is the "law" being referred to in verse 15? The "law" is a man made edict that forbade Jew and Gentile interaction. (See Acts 10:28) There is no "Law" found in the Torah forbidding Jewish and Gentile relationship. As a matter of fact, the verse we started with in Zechariah teaches us that the contrary is true. The "wall" that divides is a rabbinic fence (one of the eighteen edicts of Rabbi Shammai established in 20 B.C.E.) There is a place where Jew and Gentile can have interaction. Beth-El Ministries is trying to teach about that interaction and fellowship.

This Ministry, as you might imagine is very complex. Likewise, it is not at all popular among contemporary Christians who want "freedom." They want the benefits of having a relationship with G-d without being responsible for their actions and lifestyle. I do not for the first instant believe that this is what Yeshua or Shaul (Paul) was teaching. Yeshua clearly taught – if you love me keep my commandments. (Yochanan {John} 14:21) Keeping commandments does not sound like the message being taught in the contemporary pulpit. I realize that I have rattled on a bit. So please forgive me. I am very passionate about this message and ministry.

There was no need for Dr. Walter Oakley to apologize. By time he was finished, I had been moved so deeply by his insight and passion that I hardly knew what to say. After his response, I thanked him for his time and assistance. Because of distance and scheduling issues, this was the only interview conducted via the Internet. Even so, it was one of the best of the conversations and interviews I have had the pleasure of conducting.

Wow! Dr. Oakley has hit the nail on the head. As a community of faith, God has given us a tremendous amount of freedom, knowledge and understanding, through the revelation of His word and the operation of the gifts. But the Bible says "to whom much is given, much is required, therefore, with great freedom comes great responsibility. We must realize then what the purpose of revelation is. Revelation is for restoration; to put things back in divine order. Throughout the history of Judaism and Christianity alike, every impartation of God's grace has been a measure of restoration. The ultimate goal of restoration through revelation is to bring us to the full measure of Christ. And with out revelation, there will be no restoration.

First and foremost, that responsible freedom means we must once again begin to preach holiness and to live lives worthy of the one who has called us. Secondly, Isaiah 58:6-11 paints a vivid picture of what life will be like for believers who walk in responsible freedom. The results of responsible freedom are demonstrated as we become yielded vessels for God's mercy and grace. The portrait and ministry of such a vessel is revealed in Isaiah 58:12, *"Those from among you shall build the old waste places; you shall raise up the foundations of many generations; and you shall be called the Repairer of the Breach, the Restorer of Streets to Dwell In."*

How amazing is that? We have been called for just such a time as this, to become known as "The Repairer of the Breach" and "the Restorer of Streets to Dwell In." What breach you ask? I believe that charismatic believers have the opportunity to become repairers of the Great Breach of Christianity. "What streets?" you ask. I believe they include the streets of Jerusalem. We have been given the opportunity as a community of faith, as the Church and as a nation, to participate in God's end time plan for Israel. The Bible says that we are to become known as "the Restorers of the Streets to Dwell In."

Please understand that I am not implying that we must become Jewish. That's not the goal! The goal is to restore the broken relationship. Some will ask how this can be done. The answer is simple. It is through the gift of love which is the greatest charismatic gift of all! But not just any kind of love; it must be Agape love (Gods kind of love). That is the love by which others will know that we are His disciples. Therefore, we are presented with yet another challenge. It is the challenge to become some of the greatest peacemakers of our time by yielding to the call to embrace our Jewish brothers and sisters; to embrace the Hebraic Heritage, from which the Christian Church was born; and to embrace the truth about the future of the nation of Israel.

This challenge may require that we reject hundreds and even thousands of years of historical teachings and traditions, to be receptive to some Hebraic teachings and traditions. It will mean that we must accept what God has spoken regarding the future fate of Israel, and begin to say what God said about the Jewish nation. We are the ones who were grafted into the eternal covenant made with Israel. And if we as gentiles have been grafted in, how much more are they able to be grafted in again; by the God who has called us all by one name and joined us as one family to the single Root of Christ the Messiah. Therefore, the charismatic community has been given the golden opportunity to participate in the greatest ministry of reconciliation of our time. It is the reconciliation of the Christian Church with its Jewish heritage once again in one faith in Christ.

Chapter Fifteen
FAITH FOR THE CHALLENGE AHEAD

So there you have it. The charismatic movement has been a true blessing to the body of Christ. I wanted to share my testimony with others, because God has richly blessed my life through charismatic ministries. I asked a few friends and colleagues to help me tell the story of where we've been, where we are and what direction we may be headed. As we look to the future, we are faced with a challenge of epic and even biblical proportion. That challenge is to remain relevant to the plan of God and useful in His ministry in the end times.

But what better community of faith is there to take on that challenge than the Word of Faith and charismatic community of faith. For it is to this community that the message has been preached, "With God all things are possible" and that "Nothing is impossible to him that believes." It is in the times when we are faced with impossible odds and it appears that we have the least possible chance for success, God loves to show up and show Him self strong on our behalf.

Consider Elijah and the challenge he faced when he encountered the prophets of Baal in 1 Kings 18:20- 40. Although Elijah was unpopular and out numbered, the man of faith proved to every one of his adversaries that nothing is too hard for God. Consider also the testimony of Joshua, who was called to lead a great host of people into a land occupied by his enemies. Nevertheless he was instructed in Joshua 1:7 to *"Only be strong and very courageous."* He too was successful in his effort to overcome impossible odds as he took on the challenge of obedience. By faith he dispossessed the enemy and led the children of Israel to victory in the Promised Land. These are just a couple of examples of men of faith who took on the challenge of their day and prevailed despite the odds.

Therefore, even though the Church may be facing its most critical hour, we must understand that the members of the Word of Faith community have been chosen for such a time as this. Over the course of our discussion, we have learned that we have been called to be agents of change for the Glory of God and for the good of those around us. We made mention of the gifts and contributions God has given to the body Christ through the Word of Faith and Charismatic Movement. We've learned how the gift of teaching in particular, has impacted the Universal Church the world over. And we have been given a very special gift of music through the creation of a brand new style and genre, know as Worship and Praise music.

When it comes to questions regarding the credibility of what we believe, we discovered that charismatic Christians have just as much evidence to support their position in the faith as any other camp. And maybe even more! It just takes a little effort to uncover the biblical and historical and archeological evidence. We even learned that there is a term for the process of debating such issues in the faith. It is a skill that we too can master as we engage in the art of charismatic Christian apologetics. However, it is not our intention to strive for vain recognition or contention; but rather to pursue peace through communication. And to provide encouragement and support for those who have been discouraged and wounded by the attacks of others upon our charismatic faith.

We are again challenged to fight the good fight of faith, with the intention of winning the prize of victory which is in Christ Jesus. We must understand however, that our enemy is not the brother or sister by whom we are challenged, but rather our enemies are the world, the flesh and the devil. For this reason we must remember that we are all on the same team. And our prayer is that members of the evangelical community will realize that God has called us to become united in the faith. No matter what team God has placed you on and what job He has given you to do; we are all kingdom kids, working toward the same goal, in one Spirit, under one Lord, in one faith and in one baptism.

However, after taking a long hard look at our selves through the mirror of God's word, we find that there are major areas that need to be addressed in the charismatic community. We have acknowledged that we must legitimately consider the charges leveled against us. It is not enough to be anointed and gifted. We must be responsible for living a holy and acceptable life that is pleasing to God. Therefore, we can no long tolerate the "Sloppy Agape" approach to charismatic Christian living. This approach has cost so many of our men and women of God to be discredited and disqualified in the faith. It has also cost them the loss of God's anointing upon their ministry. If we want to remain a valuable and effective instrument in God's plan for ministry to the church and the world, then we must deal with every weight and sin that does so easily beset us. Although some may feel that it is too late for the Charismatic Movement, I for one do not believe that is the case. But I do believe that now is the time that we must make some necessary changes. God is calling us to repentance and restoration. That is the word of faith for our day.

I am convinced that God is not through with us yet! He still has a purpose and plan for members of the charismatic community. We can still be used as vessels of honor for end time ministry. Although the sun has set upon the hay day of the Charismatic Movement, it does not mean that we can not be an integral part of the next great move of God. And I believe that next move will have something to do with the Jewish people and the nation of Israel. It is quite possible that the simultaneous birth of the Charismatic Movement and the birth of the nation of Israel and the subsequent capture of Jerusalem are more than just a coincidence.

If in fact, our destiny is divinely linked, then we have come full circle in our relationship with Israel. And part of that relationship means that we must act as ambassadors of peace. God is turning the heart of the Church toward its Hebraic roots. As He does so, we are to become the change agents for our day, as we pray for the peace of Jerusalem. As change agents, God is calling us to be the Repairer of the Breach between Christianity and Judaism. We are to be known as the Restorer of the Streets to Dwell In. I believe that this is the direction for the Charismatic Church in end time ministry.

And lastly, we have learned that there is a price for freedom. God is calling us to become responsible with the knowledge and freedom we have been given. Again, to whom much is given, much is required. Therefore, we must be willing to take on the challenges ahead with the faith and courage instilled in use through the message of faith we preach. We have been called to the ministry of reconciliation. That reconciliation includes the greatest challenge of the Christian faith; it is the challenge to facilitate the reconciliation of the Christian faith with its Jewish heritage. Although the challenge may seem to be an impossible task, the scriptures tell us that nothing is impossible to him that believes. Therefore, even as God prepared Queen Esther, we too have been groomed by God for such a time as this.

Yes! I know that this may be a daunting task, but what better group of Christians to take on the challenge than the recipients of the Word of Faith message. What better community of faith than those gifted members who have experienced the charismatic grace of God? This ministry has been a positive influence upon my life and has helped to shape my life in Christ tremendously. It has also touched and shaped the lives of many other Christians I know. And despite the negative aspects of the movement, the overall impact and influence upon the body of Christ has been positive as well. After all the bad press of recent times, I felt it was time for someone to speak up and speak out, in defense of the Word of Faith. My prayer is that you have been encouraged and strengthened through the testimonies and information we've shared, as I have discussed the lessons I have learned as an Orthodox-Charismatic-Evangelical-Hebraic-Messianic Christian.

Perhaps the greatest lesson I have learned from the Word of Faith community is that these titles really do not matter. What matters most is that I am a blood bought, born again believer in Jesus Christ. In the end, that is all that matters. That is the ultimate massage and goal of the Charismatic Movement. It has been instrumental in fulfilling the purpose and prayer of our Lord. He has used this community to bring salvation to the masses and unity in the body of Christ, through the gifts that each and every joint supplies. And that may be the greatest contribution of all.

BIBLIOGROPHY AND RESOURCES CITED

"Harald Bredesen." South California Christian News 29 Dec. 2006. 20 June 2008 <www.sccn.com/Harald Bredesen.html>.

Holy Bible, Open Bible, NKJV. Nashville: Thomas Nelson Inc, 1982.

Strong, James. Vine, W. E., The New Strong's Concise Concordance & Vine's Concise Dictionary of the Bible, Nashville, Thomas Nelson, 1997

Theisen, Jerome. "Saint Benedict of Nursia." The Modern Catholic Encyclopedia, 1995. Liturgical P. 1 Apr. 2008 <http://www.osb. org/gen/benedict.html>.

Wigglesworth, Smith. Ever Increasing Faith, New Kensington: Whitaker House, 2001

Sproul, R. C. "Recovering the Beauty of the Arts." Renewing Your Mind, Ligonier Ministries, 2003

"Is American Christianity Turning Charismatic?" The Barna Group, Jan. 7, 2008. 29 Jan. 2008 <http://www.barna.org/FlexPage.aspx?Page=BarnaUpdate&BarnaUpdat eID=287>

Biema, David Van Chu, Jeff. "Does God Want You To Be Rich?" TIME Magazine (U.S. Edition), Sept. 18, 2006. Vol.168, No.12

Oakley, Walter Jr. The Jewishness of Jesus, Norris City: American Mission Teams, Inc., 2002

Oakley, Walter Jr. The Jewishness of Jesus, Beth Yeshua Ministries, 1994

Collins, Kenneth "Architecture and Furnishings." Church Architecture Glossary, Rev. Kenneth W. Collins Web Site, 1995-2008 <http://www.kencollins.com/glossary/architecture.htm>

Roman Swords, RealArmorofGod.com, Optimus International Inc., 2005 <http://www.realarmorofgod.com/roman-swords-info.html>

Reid, Amy. Kithcart, David. Harald Bredesen: A Passion for Christ, CBN-700 Club, 2007
<http://www.cbn.com/700club/features/Harald_Bredesen0307.aspx>

Barna, George. The Second Coming of the Church, Nashville: Word Publishing, a unit of Thomas Nelson Inc., 1998

The World Book Dictionary (a Thorndike-Barnhart Dictionary), Doubleday & Company Inc., 1986 ISBN: 0-7166-0286-5

Burgess, Stanley M. & van der Maas, Eduard M.. The New Dictionary of Pentecostal and Charismatic Movements, Grand Rapids: Zondervan, 2002, 2003

Moynahan, Brian. The Faith; A History of Christianity, Doubleday, 2002. ISBN 0-385-49114-X

Simple English Wikipedia, Free Software Foundation, Boston: 2002
http://simple.wikipedia.org/wiki/Dictionary

denomination. (2008). In Merriam-Webster Online Dictionary. Retrieved August 8, 2008, from http://www.merriam-webster.com/dictionary/denomination

The American Heritage® Dictionary of the English Language, Fourth Edition Copyright © 2007, 2000 by Houghton Mifflin Company. Updated in 2007. Published by Houghton Mifflin Company. All rights reserved.

Footnotes

[1] Wigglesworth, Smith. Ever Increasing Faith, New Kensington: Whitaker House, 2001. Pg10

[2] Reid, Amy. Kithcart, David. "Harald Bredesen: A Passion for Christ," CBN-700 Club, 2007

[3] "In Honor of Harald Bredesen." Square No More Press Release, Friday, December 29, 2006, @http://squarenomore.blogspot.com/2006/12/in-honor-of-harald-bredesen.html

[4] "Harald Bredesen." South California Christian News 29 Dec. 2006. <www.sccn.com/Harald Bredesen.html>

[5] Burgess, Stanley. Van der Maas, Eduard M. The New International Dictionary of Pentecostal and Charismatic Movements, Grand Rapids: Zondervan, 2002, 2003, pg. 479

[6] denomination (2008). In *Merriam-Webster Online Dictionary. Retrieved August 8, 2008, from http://www.merriam-webster.com/ dictionary/denomination*

[7] From the Simple English Wikipedia, Free Software Foundation, Boston: 2002 http://simple.wikipedia.org/wiki/Dictionary

[8] Hart, D. G., "Denominationalism: Definition and Much More from Answers.com

[9] Cavert, Samuel McCrea. *The American Churches in the Ecumenical Movement, 1900-1968*. New York: Association Press, 1968

[10] Sproul, R.C., Recovering the Beauty of the Arts, Renewing Your Mind: Ligonier Ministries, 2003, Audio Series

[11] Theisen, Jerome. "Saint Benedict of Nursia." The Modern Catholic Encyclopedia. 1995.

[12] http://www.osb.org/gen/benedict.html

[13] The World Book Dictionary (a Thorndike-Barnhart Dictionary), Doubleday & Company, Inc., 1986. ISBN 0-7166-0286-5

[14] Vine's Concise Dictionary of the Bible, Thomas Nelson Inc., 1997, 1999

[15] The Faith; A History of Christianity by Brian Moynahan, Doubleday, 2002, pg 304

[16] Biema, David Van Chu, Jeff. "Does God Want You To Be Rich?" TIME Magazine (U.S. Edition), Sept. 18, 2006. Vol.168, No.12

[17] Roman Swords, RealArmorofGod.com, Optimus International Inc., 2005. <http://www.realarmorofgod.com/roman-swords-info.html>

[18] The Barna Update, "Is American Christianity Turning Charismatic?" The Barna Group, Jan. 7, 2008

[19] Note: The omitting of the letter "o" is a reverential Jewish practice intended to honor the Holiness of God.

[20] **Marcion** (ca. 110-160) was a Christian theologian who was excommunicated by the early Christian church at Rome as a heretic. He propounded a Christianity free from Jewish doctrines with Paul as the reliable source of authentic doctrine. (See Wikipedia article, "Marcion of Sonope", http://en.wikipedia.org/wiki/Marcion)

Made in the USA
Lexington, KY
01 July 2012